Teacher Edition

Reveal MATH™ Accelerated

Language Development Handbook

Mc Graw Hill

my.mheducation.com

Send all inquiries to:
McGraw-Hill Education
STEM Learning Solutions Center
8787 Orion Place
Columbus, OH 43240

ISBN: 978-0-07-681957-7 *(Language Development Handbook, Reveal Math Accelerated, Teacher Edition)*
MHID: 0-07-681957-4 *(Language Development Handbook, Reveal Math Accelerated, Teacher Edition)*
ISBN: 978-0-07-681956-0 *(Language Development Handbook, Reveal Math Accelerated, Student Edition)*
MHID: 0-07-681956-6 *(Language Development Handbook, Reveal Math Accelerated, Student Edition)*

Visual Kinesthetic Vocabulary® is a registered trademark of
Dinah-Might Adventures, LP.

1 2 3 4 5 6 7 8 9 10 LMN 28 27 26 25 24 23 22 21 20 19

Contents

Module 6 Algebraic Expressions

Module 7 Equations and Inequalities

Module 8 Linear Relationships and Slope

Module 9 Probability

Module 10 Sampling and Statistics

Module 11 Geometric Figures

Module 12 Area, Surface Area, and Volume

Module 13 Transformations, Congruence, and Similarity

McGraw-Hill Education's Guiding Principles for Supporting English Learners

McGraw-Hill Education is committed to providing English Learners appropriate support as they simultaneously learn content and language. As an organization, we recognize that the United States is a culturally and linguistically diverse country. Moreover, this diversity continues to increase, with corresponding growth in the number of English Learners (ELLs). In 2012–2013, an estimated 4.85 million ELLs were enrolled US schools; this subgroup now makes up nearly 10% of the total public school enrollment (Ruiz-Soto, Hooker, and Batalova, 2015). In fact, ELLs are the fastest growing student population in the country, growing 60% in the last decade, compared with only 7% growth of the general student population (Grantmakers for Education, 2013). Perhaps most interesting of all, the vast majority of ELLs – 85% of prekindergarten through fifth grade ELLs, and 62% of high school ELLs – were born in the United States (Zong & Batalova, 2015). These US-born ELLs may be first-, second-, or third-generation students with strong ties to their cultural roots.

A great many ELLs come to school with a variety of rich linguistic and cultural backgrounds from Spanish-speaking communities and countries all throughout the Americas. In addition to Spanish, there are some ELLs that come to school speaking fluent or limited Spanish in addition to an indigenous language native to North, Central and South America. In addition, schools experience native speakers from numerous other backgrounds and languages—the most common other languages being Cantonese, Hmong, Korean, Vietnamese, and Haitian Creole. While over 70% of ELLs come to school speaking Spanish as their native language, as a group, ELLs speak nearly 150 languages (Baird, 2015). The experiences and identities acquired in the context of ELLs' homes and communities can transform the simplest classroom into a unique cultural and linguistic microcosm.

English Learners' success in learning a second language is influenced by a variety of factors besides the instructional method itself, including individual, family, and classroom characteristics; school and community contexts; the attributes of the assessment used to measure progress; and whether the language acquired is a national or foreign language (August & Shanahan, 2006; Genesee, Lindholm-Leary, Saundes, & Christian, 2006). For instance, children's initial levels of proficiency in their home language(s), along with English, influence new language acquisition (August, Shanahan, Escamilla, K., 2009) as does the quality of school support (Niehaus & Adelson, 2014) and the characteristics of the language learners' first and second languages (Dressler & Kamil, 2006)

Given these factors, there is a pressing need for fundamental principles that guide the support of ELLs as they acquire content and develop language. Drawing upon extensive research in the field, McGraw-Hill Education has developed nine guiding principles for supporting English Learners at all grade levels and in all disciplines.

Guiding Principles

- ✅ Provide Specialized Instruction

- ✅ Cultivate Meaning

- ✅ Teach Structure and Form

- ✅ Develop Language in Context

- ✅ Scaffold to Support Access

- ✅ Foster Interaction

- ✅ Create Affirming Cultural Spaces

- ✅ Engage Home to Enrich Instruction

- ✅ Promote Multilingualism

Proficiency Level Descriptors

	Interpretive (Input)		Productive (Output)	
	Listening	**Reading**	**Writing**	**Speaking**
An Entering/Emerging Level ELL • New to this country; may have memorized some everyday phrases like, "Where is the bathroom", "My name is....", may also be in the "silent stage" where they listen to the language but are not comfortable speaking aloud • Struggles to understand simple conversations • Can follow simple classroom directions when overtly demonstrated by the instructor	• Listens actively yet struggles to understand simple conversations • Possibly understands "chunks" of language; may not be able to produce language verbally	• Reads familiar patterned text • Can transfer Spanish decoding somewhat easily to make basic reading in English seem somewhat fluent; comprehension is weak	• Writes labels and word lists, copies patterned sentences or sentence frames, one- or two-word responses	• Responds non-verbally by pointing, nodding, gesturing, drawing • May respond with yes/no, short phrases, or simple memorized sentences • Struggles with non-transferable pronunciations.
A Developing/Expanding Level ELL • Is dependent on prior knowledge, visual cues, topic familiarity, and pretaught math-related vocabulary • Solves word problems with significant support • May procedurally solve problems with a limited understanding of the math concept.	• Has ability to understand and distinguish simple details and concepts of familiar/ previously learned topics	• Recognizes obvious cognates • Pronounces most English words correctly, reading slowly and in short phrases • Still relies on visual cues and peer or teacher assistance	• Produces writing that consists of short, simple sentences loosely connected with limited use of cohesive devices • Uses undetailed descriptions with difficulty expressing abstract concepts	• Uses simple sentence structure and simple tenses • Prefers to speak in present tense.
A Bridging Level ELL • May struggle with conditional structure of word problems • Participates in social conversations needing very little contextual support • Can mentor other ELLs in collaborative activities.	• Usually understands longer, more elaborated directions, conversations, and discussions on familiar and some unfamiliar topics • May struggle with pronoun usage	• Reads with fluency, and is able to apply basic and higher-order comprehension skills when reading grade-appropriate text	• Is able to engage in writing assignments in content area instruction with scaffolded support • Has a grasp of basic verbs, tenses, grammar features, and sentence patterns	• Participates in most academic discussions on familiar topics, with some pauses to restate, repeat, or search for words and phrases to clarify meaning.

Collaborative Conversations

Students engage in whole-class, small-group, and partner discussions during every lesson. The chart below provides prompt frames and response frames that will help students at different language proficiency levels interact with each other in meaningful ways.

You may wish to post these frames in the classroom for student reference.

Core Skills	Prompt Frames	Response Frames
Elaborate and Ask Questions	Can you tell me more about it? Can you give me some details? Can you be more specific? What do you mean by...? How or why is it important?	I think it means that... In other words... It's important because... It's similar to when...
Support Ideas with Evidence	Can you give any examples from the text? What are some examples from other texts? What evidence do you see for that? How can you justify that idea? Can you show me where the text says that?	The text says that... An example from another text is... According to... Some evidence that supports that is...
Build On or Challenge Partner's Ideas	What do you think of the idea that...? Can we add to this idea? Do you agree? What are other ideas/points of view? What else do we need to think about? How does that connect to the idea...?	I would add that... I want to follow up on your idea... Another way to look at it is... What you said made me think of...
Paraphrase	What do we know so far? To recap, I think that... I'm not sure that was clear. How can we relate what I said to the topic/question?	So, you are saying that... Let me see if I understand you... Do you mean that...? In other words... It sounds like you are saying that...
Determine the Main Idea and Key Details	What have we discussed so far? How can we summarize what we have talked about? What can we agree upon? What are main points or ideas we can share? What relevant details support the main points or ideas? What key ideas can we take away?	We can say that... The main idea seems to be... As a result of this conversation, we think that we should... The evidence suggests that...

Strategies for Classroom Discussion

Providing multiple opportunities to speak in the classroom and welcoming all levels of participation will motivate English learners to take part in class discussions and build oral proficiency. These basic teaching strategies will encourage whole class and small group discussions for all language proficiency levels of English learners.

 Wait time/Different Response

- Be sure to give students enough time to answer the question. They may need more time to process their ideas.
- Let them know that they can respond in different ways depending on their levels of proficiency. Students can:
  - Answer in their native language; then you can rephrase in English
  - Ask a more proficient ELL speaker to repeat the answer in English
  - Answer with nonverbal cues.

 Elaborate

- If students give a one-word answer or a nonverbal clue, elaborate on the answer to model fluent speaking and grammatical patterns.
- Provide more examples or repeat the answer using proper academic language.

 Elicit

- Prompt students to give a more comprehensive response by asking additional questions or guiding them to get an answer, such as can you tell me more?
- This strategy is very effective when students are asked to justify or explain their reasoning.

 Asking about Meaning

- Repeating an answer offers an opportunity to clarify the meaning of a response.
- Repeating an answer allows you to model the proper form for a response. You can model how to answer in full sentences and use academic language.
- When you repeat the answer, correct any grammar or pronunciation errors.

ENTERING/EMERGING

- What is _____?
- What does _____ mean?
- _____ is _____.
- _____ means _____.

DEVELOPING/EXPANDING

- Could you tell me what _____ means?
- _____ is similar to _____.
- _____ is another way of saying _____.

BRIDGING

- Could you give me a definition of _____?
- Can you point to the evidence from the text?
- What is the best answer? Why?

Talk about Level of Understanding

ENTERING/EMERGING
- I understand./I got it.
- I don't understand this word/sentence.

DEVELOPING/EXPANDING
- Could you tell me what _____ means?
- _____ is another way of saying _____.

BRIDGING
- I think I understand most of it.
- I'm not sure I understand this completely.

 Justify Your Reasoning

ENTERING/EMERGING
- I think _____.

DEVELOPING/EXPANDING
- My reasons are _____.

BRIDGING
- I think _____ because _____.

 Agreeing with Someone's Reasoning

ENTERING/EMERGING
- I agree with your reasons or point.

DEVELOPING/EXPANDING
- I agree that _____.

BRIDGING
- I have the same reasons as _____. I think that _____.

Disagreeing with Someone's Reasoning

ENTERING/EMERGING
- I don't agree with your reasons.

DEVELOPING/EXPANDING
- I don't agree that _____.

BRIDGING
- I can see your point. However, I think that _____.

How to Use the Teacher Edition

The suggested strategies, activities, and tips provide additional language and concept support to accelerate English learners' acquisition of academic English.

English Learner Instructional Strategy

Each English Learner Instructional Strategy can be utilized before or during regular class instruction.

Categories of the scaffolded support are:

- Vocabulary Support
- Language Structure Support
- Sensory Support
- Graphic Support
- Collaborative Support

The goal of the scaffolding strategies is to make each individual lesson more comprehensible for ELLs by providing visual, contextual and linguistic support to foster students' understanding of basic communication in an academic context.

Lesson 1 Unit Rates Involving Complex Fractions

English Learner Instructional Strategy

Vocabulary Support: Frontload Academic Vocabulary

Before the lesson, write and discuss these multiple-meaning words: *complex* and *reciprocal*. Define each word, using realia, demonstrations, and illustrations to support understanding.

Complex fractions are simplified when the numerator and denominator are both integers. Write the word *integer*. Explain that an integer can be either positive or negative. Draw a number line numbered from −5 to 5. Then read aloud each number as you point to it. Explain that each number is an integer because it does not include a fraction or decimal amount. Then point to the negative signs that precede −5 through −1. Explain how the signs show that these numbers are negative, or less than zero, and how numbers without a negative sign

Since ELLs benefit from visual references to new vocabulary, many of the English Learner Instruction Strategies suggest putting vocabulary words on a Word Wall. Choose a location in your classroom for your Word Wall, and organize the words by module, by topic, or alphabetically.

English Language Development Leveled Activities

These activities are tiered for Entering/Emerging, Developing/ Expanding, and Bridging leveled ELLs. Activity suggestions are specific to the content of the lesson. Some activities include instruction to support students with lesson specific vocabulary they will need to understand the math content in English, while other activities teach the concept or skill using scaffolded approaches specific to ELLs. The activities are intended for small group instruction, and can be directed by the instructor, an aide, or a peer mentor.

English Language Development Leveled Activities

Entering/Emerging	Developing/Expanding	Bridging
Word Knowledge	**Anchor Chart**	**Partners Work/Pairs Check**
Write: $2 \cdot 2 \cdot 5 = 20$ and *factored form*. Underline *factor*. Point to 2 and ask, *Is 2 a factor?* **yes** Repeat with 5. Point to 20 and ask, *Is 20 a factor?* **no** Help students define *factor*. Then circle the *ed* in *factore*[... *Teacher talk is italicized.* ...] the -e[... ...] noun i[...]o an a[...]is a describing [...]. Show and explain how *factored* describes *form*: The *factored form* of an expression is the *form* that shows its *factors*. Finally, write expressions in both their factored and unfactored forms. Ask, *Which is the factored form?* Students point to the answer.	Draw a four-column chart on the board, with these column heads: Factor (noun), Factor (verb), Factored Form, Greatest Common Factor. Then, under each head, have students help you write the following: 1) a math definition for the term, using students' words; 2)[... *Student talk is boldfaced.* ...]rm in [...]e. [...] responses for the noun *factor*: **1) Definition: a number or variable multiplied by another number or variable to form a product; 2) One factor of 21 is 7; 3) Factors of 21 are 1, 3, 7, 21.**	Have partners work together to write word problems involving monomials. Tell them their word problems must include information that can be represented in a linear expression and a solution that involves factoring the expression. Then have students trade their problems with another pair and solve the word problem they receive. Finally, have partners check answers with the pair who wrote the problem.

Multicultural Teacher Tip

You may see some ELLs using a method other than the factor trees commonly used in U.S. classrooms to find factors. In Mexico, students are taught to draw a vertical line. On the left side, they write the number to be factored, and then the first prime factor is written on the [...]

18	2
9	3

Multicultural Teacher Tip

These tips provide insight on academic and cultural differences you may encounter in your classroom. While math is the universal language, some ELLs may have been shown different methods to find the answer based on their native country, while cultural customs may influence learning styles and behavior in the classroom.

How to Use the Student Edition

Each student page provides ELL support for vocabulary, note taking, and writing skills. These pages can be used before, during, or after classroom instruction. A corresponding page with answers is found in the teacher resources.

Word Cards

Students define each vocabulary word or phrase and write a sentence using the term in context. Space is provided for Spanish speakers to write the definition in Spanish.

A blank word card template is provided for use with non-Spanish speaking ELLs.

Lesson 4 Vocabulary
Discounts

Use the word cards to define each vocabulary word or phrase and give an example.

Word Cards

discount

Definition

descuento

Definición

Example Sentence

Copyright © McGraw-Hill Education

Vocabulary Squares

Vocabulary squares reinforce the lesson vocabulary by having students write a definition, write a sentence using the vocabulary in context, and create an example of the vocabulary. Suggest that students use translation tools and write notes in English or in their native language on the cards as well for clarification of terms. Encourage students to identify and make note of cognates to help accelerate the acquisition of math concepts in English.

Lesson 1 Vocabulary
Rational Numbers

Use the vocabulary squares to write a definition, a sentence, and an example for each vocabulary word.

repeating decimal	Definition
Example	Sentence

bar notation	Definition
Example	Sentence

Three-Column Chart

Three-column charts concentrate on English/Spanish cognates. Students are given the word in English. Encourage students to use a glossary to find the word in Spanish and the definition in English. As an extension, have students identify and highlight other cognates which may be in the definitions.

A blank three-column chart template is provided for use with non-Spanish speaking ELLs.

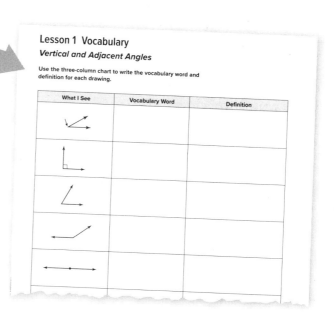

Lesson 1 Vocabulary
Vertical and Adjacent Angles

Use the three-column chart to write the vocabulary word and definition for each drawing.

What I See	Vocabulary Word	Definition

Lesson 2 Vocabulary
Area of Circles

Use the definition map to list qualities about the vocabulary word or phrase.

Vocabulary

semicircle

Description

Characteristics

Draw examples of semicircles.

Definition Map

The definition maps are designed to address a single vocabulary word, phrase, or concept. Students should define the word in the description box. Most definition maps will ask students to list characteristics and examples. Others, as shown at the left, will ask students to perform other tasks. Make sure you review with students the tasks required.

How to Use the Student Edition *continued*

Concept Web

Concept webs are designed to show relationships between concepts and to make connections. Encourage students to find examples or words they can use in the web.

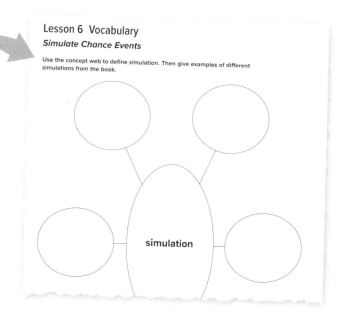

Lesson 6 Vocabulary
Simulate Chance Events

Use the concept web to define simulation. Then give examples of different simulations from the book.

simulation

Cornell Notes

Cornell notes provide students with a method to take notes thereby helping them with language structure. Scaffolded sentence frames are provided for students to fill-in important math vocabulary by identifying the correct word or phrase according to context.

Lesson 3 Notetaking
Subtract Linear Expressions

Use Cornell notes to better understand the lesson's concepts. Complete each sentence by filling in the blanks with the correct word or phrase.

Questions	Notes
1. How do I subtract linear expressions?	I subtract _____ terms. I use _____ pairs if needed.
2. What is the additive inverse of a linear expression?	The additive inverse of a linear expression is an expression with terms that are _____. The sum of a linear expression and its additive inverse is _____.

English/Spanish Cognates used in *Reveal Math Accelerated*

English	Spanish	VKV Page Number
absolute value	valor absoluto	VKV7
acute triangle	triángulo acutángulo	
additive inverse	inverso aditivo	VKV7
algebra	álgebra	
algebraic expression	expresión algebraica	
alternate exterior angles	ángulos alternos externos	
alternate interior angles	ángulos alternos internos	
Associative Property	propiedad asociativa	
bar notation	notación de barra	VKV13
base	base	VKV16
center	centro	VKV37
center of rotation	centro de rotación	VKV57
circle	circulo	VKV37
circumference	circunferencia	VKV37
coefficient	coeficiente	VKV19, VKV25
common denominator	común denominador	VKV13
Commutative Property	propiedad conmutativa	
complementary angles	ángulos complementarios	
complementary events	eventos complementarios	
composite figure	figura compuesto	VKV39
composition of transformations	composición de transformaciones	
compound event/simple event	evento compuesto/evento simple	
cone	cono	VKV43, VKV49
congruent	congruente	VKV53
constant	constante	
constant of proportionality	constante de proporcionalidad	
constant of variation	constante de variación	
corresponding angles	ángulos correspondientes	
cylinder	cilindro	VKV43, VKV49
define a variable	definir una variable	
dimensional analysis	análisis dimensional	
direct variation	variación directa	
Distributive Property	propiedad distributiva	
equation	ecuación	
equilateral triangle	triángulo equilátero	
equivalent equation	ecuación equivalente	VKV23
experimental probability/theoretical probability	probabilidad experimental/probabilidad teórica	VKV31

English	Spanish	VKV Page Number
exponent	exponente	VKV16
exterior angles	ángulo externo	
factor	factorizar	VKV19
factored form	forma factorizada	VKV19
graph	graficar	VKV11
hemisphere	hemisferio	VKV51
identity	identidad	VKV25
image	imagen	
interior angles	ángulos internos	
irrational number	número irracional	VKV15
isosceles triangle	triángulo isosceles	
lateral surface area	área de superficie lateral	VKV41
line of reflection	linea de reflexión	VKV55
linear equation	ecuación lineal	
linear expression	expresión lineal	VKV21
linear relationship	relación lineal	VKV27
monomial	monomio	VKV21
Multiplicative Identity Property	propiedad de identidad de la multiplicación	
multiplicative inverse	inversos multiplicativo	VKV25
negative	negativo	
nonproportional/proportional	no proporcional/proporcional	
obtuse angle	ángulo obtuso	
obtuse triangle	triángulo obtuso	
opposites	opuestos	VKV11
ordered pair	par ordenado	
origin	origen	
percent error	porcentaje de error	VKV5
perfect cube	cubo perfecto	VKV17
plane	plano	VKV43
population	población	VKV33
preimage	preimagen	VKV53
prism	prisma	
probability	probabilidad	
properties	propiedades	
property	propiedad	
proportion	proporción	VKV3
pyramid	pirámide	
radical sign	signo radical	VKV17
radius/diameter	radio/diámetro	VKV39

English	Spanish	VKV Page Number
rational number	número racional	VKV9, VKV16
real numbers	número reales	
reflection	reflexión	
regular polygon	polígono regular	VKV47
regular pyramid	pirámide regular	VKV45
relative frequency	frecuencia relative	
rotation	rotación	
scale	escala	
scale factor	factor de escala	VKV36
scale model	modelo a escala	VKV19
scalene triangle	triángulo escaleno	
scientific notation	notación científica	VKV17
semicircle	semicirculo	VKV39
similar	similar	
simple interest	interés simple	
simplify	simplificar	
simulation	simulación	VKV29
solution	solución	VKV23
sphere	esfera	VKV51
statistics	estadística	VKV33
supplementary angles	ángulos suplementarios	
surface area	área de superficie	
term	término	
transformation	transformación	VKV55
translation	traslación	VKV53
transversal	transversal	
triangle	triángulo	VKV47
uniform probability model	modelo de probabilidad uniforme	
vertex	vértice	
volume	volumen	
x-coordinate/y-coordinate	coordenada x/coordenada y	
y-intercept	intersección y	

Lesson _____

Use the word cards to define each vocabulary word or phrase and give an example.

Word Cards

Definition

_____

_____

_____

Example Sentence

_____

_____

- -

Word Cards

Definition

_____

_____

_____

Example Sentence

_____

_____

Lesson _____

Use the three-column chart to organize the vocabulary in this lesson.

English	Native Language	Definition

Lesson 1 Unit Rates Involving Ratios of Fractions

English Learner Instructional Strategy

Vocabulary Support: Frontload Academic Vocabulary

Before the lesson, write and discuss these multiple-meaning words: *complex* and *reciprocal*. Define each word, using realia, demonstrations, and illustrations to support understanding.

Complex fractions are simplified when the numerator and denominator are both integers. Write the word *integer*. Explain that an integer can be either positive or negative. Draw a number line numbered from −5 to 5. Then read aloud each number as you point to it. Explain that each number is an integer because it does not include a fraction or decimal amount. Then point to the negative signs that precede −5 through −1. Explain how the signs show that these numbers are negative, or less than zero, and how numbers without a negative sign are positive, or greater than zero or zero.

English Language Development Leveled Activities

Entering/Emerging	Developing/Expanding	Bridging
Developing Oral Language List the following items: $\frac{8}{2}$; $8 \div 2$; 8 divided by 2. Then point to each and say, *All of these mean the same thing.* In the first item, point to 8 and say *eight,* point to the fraction bar and say *divided by,* then point to 2 and say *two.* Repeat the process with the other two items. Then ask, *What is eight divided by two?* Have students respond using this sentence frame: _____ **divided by** _____ **equals** _____. Now write: $\frac{9}{3}$; $9 \div 3$; 9 divided by 3. Have students say each expression and then say its solution using the sentence frame.	**Building Oral Language** Write the following: $\frac{\frac{1}{4}}{2}$ and $\frac{1}{4} \div 2$. Point to both items and say, *These mean the same thing.* In Item 1, point first to $\frac{1}{4}$ and say *one-fourth,* then to the larger fraction bar and say *divided by,* finally point to 2 and say *two.* Next, in Item 2, point first to $\frac{1}{4}$ and say *one-fourth,* then to the division sign and say *divided by,* finally point to 2 and say *two.* Now say, *Let's simplify the expresison.* Work through the steps to simplify the complex fraction. Have students respond, using this sentence frame: _____ **divided by** _____ **is the same as** _____ **times** _____. **The answer is** _____.	**Think-Pair-Share** Have partners work together to write a word problem whose solution involves dividing one fraction by another fraction. If students have difficulty writing a problem, refer them back to Examples 3-5 in the book. Then ask students to exchange problems with another pair. Have partners work together to solve the problem they received. Then ask them to present the word problem and solution to the class. Allow peers to ask questions and have the presenter justify their solution.

Teacher Notes:

NAME _____ DATE _____ PERIOD _____

Lesson 1 Vocabulary

Unit Rates Involving Ratios of Fractions

Use the definition map to list qualities about the vocabulary word or phrase.
Sample answers are given.

Vocabulary

> **complex fraction**

Characteristics

> both the numerator and the denominator can be fractions

> in simplest form when the numerator and denominator are integers

Description

> a fraction where the numerator and/or denominator are fractions

$$\frac{\frac{1}{2}}{\frac{1}{5}} = \frac{5}{2} \text{ or } 2\frac{1}{2} \qquad \frac{9}{\frac{3}{4}} = 12$$

Write and simplify examples of complex fractions.

Module 1 *Proportional Relationships*   **1**

Lesson 2 Understand Proportional Relationships

English Learner Instructional Strategy

Language Structure Support: Tiered Responses

As you work through the lesson, be sure to check ELL students' understanding during every step. You can do this by asking questions that elicit responses appropriate to their level of English acquisition. Instructions for Entering/Emerging students must be short and clear, using known vocabulary, so they can respond by pointing or saying **yes/no**. Developing/Expanding students can give short answers and may attempt simple sentences. Bridging students can create longer sentences and synthesize more information in English.

Emerging/Emerging students: *Point to the square that shows 1 part. Does this show a proportional relationship?*
Developing/Expanding students: *How many parts of _____? How many equal sections? How many ___ does each section represent?*
Bridging students: *What is the ratio of ___ to ___? How do you know this is a proportional relationship?*

English Language Development Leveled Activities

Entering/Emerging	Developing/Expanding	Bridging
Listen and Identify	Act It Out	Anchor Chart
Invite four students to come forward. Hand each student one pencil. Then hand each student three sheets of paper. On the board, draw a table showing the ratio of 1 pencil to 3 sheets of paper. Say, *This is a proportional relationship*. Have students chorally repeat **proportional relationship**. Then hand each student between one and four paper clips. Draw a table showing that the number of paper clips per student is a nonproportional relationship. Say, *This is a nonproportional relationship. It is **not** proportional.* Have students chorally repeat **nonproportional relationship**.	On the board, draw a table showing the ratio 1:5. Divide students into small groups of three or four students and distribute manipulatives to each group. Have them use manipulatives to show a proportional relationship, with 1 part equal to 6. Then ask, *How many are in 5 parts?* **30** Then have students use the manipulatives to show a nonproportional relationship, or a ratio that is not equivalent to 1:5. Have students use the following sentence frames to explain their nonproportional example: **The ratio ___ to ___ is not equivalent to one to five. So it is a nonproportional relationship.**	Have students work in small groups to create anchor charts for proportional and nonproportional relationships. Their charts should include definitions and examples. Have students display their charts. Then ask one volunteer from each group to explain why their group's examples show proportional and nonproportional relationships.

Teacher Notes:

NAME _____ DATE _____ PERIOD _____

Lesson 2 Notetaking

Understand Proportional Relationships

Use Cornell notes to better understand the lesson's concepts. Complete each sentence by filling in the blanks with the correct word or phrase.

Questions	Notes
What is a proportional relationship?	Two quantities are in a _proportional relationship_ when the two quantities _vary_ and have a constant _ratio_ between them. Example: A recipe calls for 1 tablespoon of baking soda for every 4 cups of flour. Elise uses 4 tablespoons of baking soda for 16 cups of flour. Is this a proportional relationship? ┤1 tbsp├ baking soda [1] flour [1][1][1][1] ├------ 4 cups ------┤
Words I need help with: See students' words.	┤4 tbsp├ baking soda [4] flour [4][4][4][4] ├------ 16 cups ------┤ The ratio _was_ maintained, so this _is_ a proportional relationship.

Summary

What are other ways to show proportional relationships bedsides bar diagrams?

See students' examples.

_____

_____

_____

Lesson 3 Tables of Proportional Relationships

English Learner Instructional Strategy

Vocabulary Support: Activate Prior Knowledge

Before the lesson, write *proportional* and *nonproportional* and their Spanish cognates, *proporcional* and *no proporcional,* respectively, on the Word Wall. Introduce the words, and provide math examples to support understanding. Utilize other appropriate translation tools for non-Spanish speaking ELLs. Then circle *non-* in *nonproportional.* Explain that *non-* is a prefix that means "not." Point out that when *non-* is added to *proportional,* it forms a word that is an antonym of *proportional.* Then tell students that *proportional* is a multiple-meaning word. Discuss how this word is used within the context of design, as well as math.

English Language Development Leveled Activities

Use the following problem with these leveled activities: *Andrew earns $18 per hour for mowing lawns. Is the amount of money he earns proportional to the number of hours he spends mowing?*

Entering/Emerging	Developing/Expanding	Bridging
Look, Listen, and Identify	**Academic Word Knowledge**	**Show What You Know**
Write the ratios for the problem on the board and say, *This is a* **ratio**. *Each ratio compares the amount of money earned to the hours Andrew works.* Point to each ratio and say, for example, *The* **ratio** *is eighteen to one.* Have students repeat each ratio chorally, using this sentence frame: **The ratio is _____ .** Ask, *Are all of these ratios* **equivalent***, or equal?* **yes** Then circle all the ratios and say, *All of these ratios are* **equivalent***. So, the relationship between the amount of money Andrew earns to the hours he works is* **proportional***.* Have students repeat chorally.	Repeat the Emerging Level activity. Say The relationship between the cost of boxes of cards and the number of boxes purchased are shown by following ratios. Write $\frac{\$15}{1}, \frac{\$25}{2}, \frac{\$35}{3},$ and $\frac{\$45}{4}$ on the board. Ask, *Are all the ratios* **equivalent?** **no** Say, *The ratios are* **not** *equivalent, so the relationship between the cost and the number of boxes of cards is* **nonproportional***.* Have students repeat chorally.	Divide students into pairs, and give each pair an index card. Ask students to describe a relationship that is proportional and write three ratios that represent the relationship. Then have them repeat the process for a nonproportional relationship. Ask partners to present both sets to the class, explaining why each is proportional or nonproportional.

Teacher Notes:

NAME _____ DATE _____ PERIOD _____

Lesson 3 Vocabulary

Tables of Proportional Relationships

Use the three-column chart to organize the vocabulary in this lesson. Write the word in Spanish. Then write the definition of each word. Sample answers are given.

English	Spanish	Definition
proportional	proporcional	the relationship between two ratios with a constant rate or ratio
nonproportional	no proporcional	the relationship between two ratios with a rate or ratio that is not constant
constant of proportionality	constante de proporcionalidad	a constant ratio or unit rate of two variable quantities

Lesson 4 Graphs of Proportional Relationships

English Learner Instructional Strategy

Vocabulary Support: Anchor Chart

Before the lesson, add the terms *coordinate plane, ordered pair, x-coordinate, y-coordinate,* and *origin* and their Spanish cognates, *plano de coordenadas, par ordenado, coordenada* x, *coordenada* y, and *origen,* respectively, to a Word Wall. Introduce the words, and provide math examples to support understanding.

Have students preview the illustration of a four-quadrant coordinate plane on the student page. On an anchor chart, write the following associated vocabulary: *grid, intersect, quadrants, zero points, x-axis, y-axis, negative numbers, positive numbers, graph.* Use the illustration and realia, as needed, to explain each term. Then have students help you write a definition for the term to be added to the anchor chart.

English Language Development Leveled Activities

Entering/Emerging	Developing/Expanding	Bridging
Word Knowledge Draw a coordinate plane. Then write: (1, 2). Point to the numbers and say, *This is an **ordered pair.*** Have students repeat chorally. Explain that an ordered pair always appears inside parentheses. Point to the parentheses. Have students repeat chorally. Then explain how the order in which the numbers appear is important. Say, *The **first** number coordinates with the **x-axis.*** Point to the x-axis. Then say, *The **second** number coordinates with the **y-axis.*** Point to the y-axis. Show students how to use the ordered pair to plot a point on the coordinate plane.	**Show What You Know** Write the chart below on the board. | Number of Books	Number of Students
---	---
0	0
2	1
4	2
6	3 | Draw the first quadrant of a coordinate plane. Label the x-axis "Books" and the y-axis "Students." Invite volunteers to write ordered pairs based on the numbers in the chart and then plot them on the coordinate plane. Ask, *Is the number of books proportional to the number of students?* Have students respond using this sentence frame: **The number of books [is/is not] proportional to the number of students.**	**Number Game** Draw two first quadrant coordinate planes. Label the axes with increments of 5. Divide students into two teams. Have both teams face away from the board as you write these ordered pairs: (0, 0), (1, 7), (2, 14), (3, 21). Then tell students they will do a relay race: First, one student from each team plots the point described in the first ordered pair. Then that student passes the marker to a team member, to plot the point described by the next ordered pair. Students continue this way until all points are plotted. The final student correctly identifies the points' relationship by writing *proportional* or *nonproportional.* **proportional** The first team to finish wins!

Teacher Notes:

NAME _____ DATE _____ PERIOD _____

Lesson 4 Vocabulary
Graphs of Proportional Relationships

Use the word bank to identify the parts of the coordinate plane. Then draw an arrow from the word to the part of the coordinate plane it describes.

Word Bank			
origin	ordered pair	Quadrant III	Quadrant I
x-axis	*x*-coordinate	*y*-axis	*y*-coordinate

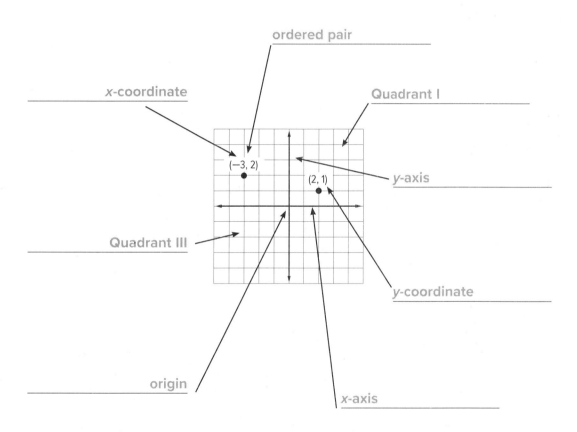

ordered pair _____

x-coordinate _____

Quadrant I _____

(−3, 2)

(2, 1)

y-axis _____

Quadrant III _____

y-coordinate _____

origin _____

x-axis _____

Lesson 5 Equations of Proportional Relationships

English Learner Instructional Strategy

Vocabulary Support: Cognates

Before the lesson, add the phrase *constant of proportionality* and the Spanish cognate, *constant de proporcionalidad*, to a Word Wall. Introduce the phrase and provide math examples to support understanding. Ask students to refer to a dictionary or glossary to recall the meaning of *constant*. Then write: *proportion/proportionality*. Explain that the first word in the pair carries the main meaning for the second word in the pair. Then help students relate the meanings of the paired words.

English Language Development Leveled Activities

Entering/Emerging	Developing/Expanding	Bridging
Anchor Chart Have students help you create an anchor chart. First, write: $\frac{y}{x}$. Ask, *What is $\frac{y}{x}$?* **a ratio** Note this on the chart. Then write: $\frac{y}{x} = k$. Say, *These symbols show a* **relationship***. What is the* **relationship** *called?* **a proportional relationship** Note this on the chart. Ask, *When $\frac{y}{x}$ equals k, what* **kind** *of ratio is $\frac{y}{x}$?* **a constant ratio** Note this on the chart. Finally, ask, *In a proportional relationship, what do we call the* **constant ratio***?* **constant of variation, constant of proportionality** Note this on the chart.	**Show What You Know** Display and read aloud this word problem: *A bird travels* y *miles in* x *hours. If y = 14x, then how far does the bird travel in 3 hours?* Then write: $\frac{y}{x} = k$. Ask, *What is another way to write this formula? Look at the word problem for a hint.* **y = kx** Then ask, *What number is constant?* **14** Next, say, *The problem says the bird travels 3 hours. Does 3 take the place of y or x in the formula?* **x** *So, what does y equal?* **42** Now write: $\frac{42 \text{ miles}}{3 \text{ hours}}$. Say, *If it takes 3 hours to travel 42 miles, what is the constant ratio?* Have students respond using this sentence frame: **The constant ratio is ____.** $\frac{14}{1}$	**Think-Pair-Share** Display and read aloud this word problem: *A bird travels* y *miles in* x *hours. If y = 14x, then how far does the bird travel in 3 hours?* Have students solve the problem independently. Then have them check their answers with a partner. As you monitor the activity, suggest students use everyday language, such as, **I agree with your answer. Your answer is not the same as mine. I think this might be wrong. Did you remember to ____ ? Why don't you try ____?** Once partners agree on an answer, invite a volunteer to share the problem's solution, along with an explanation of how the problem was solved.

Multicultural Teacher Tip

Encourage ELLs to share traditions, stories, songs, or other aspects of their native culture with the other students in class. You might even create a "culture wall" where all students can display cultural items. This will help create a classroom atmosphere of respect and appreciation for all cultures, and in turn, will create a more comfortable learning environment for students.

NAME _____ DATE _____ PERIOD _____

Lesson 5 Vocabulary
Equations of Proportional Relationships

Use the word cards to define each vocabulary word, and complete the Example
sentence. Sample answers are given.

Word Card

constant of proportionality	constant de proporcionalidad
Definition	**Definición**
a constant ratio or unit rate of two variable quantities	una razón constante o tasa por unidad de dos cantidades variables

Example

In the equation $y = kx$, the variable ___k___ represents the
constant of proportionality.

Word Card

unit rate	tasa unitaria
Definition	**Definición**
a rate that is simplified so that it has a denominator of 1 unit	tasa simplificada para que tenga un denominador igual a 1

Example

In a proportional relationship, the ___constant of proportionality___
is the same as the unit rate.

Lesson 6 Solve Problems Involving Proportional Relationships

English Learner Instructional Strategy

Vocabulary Support: Utilize Resources

Before the lesson, review the Word Wall for vocabulary introduced earlier in the lesson. In particular, point out the base word proportion that appears in some of the words and phrases they learned, such as proportional relationship and constant of proportionality. Then add proportion and its Spanish cognate, proporción, to the Word Wall. Introduce its meaning and provide examples to support understanding.

Then preview the lesson with a "chapter walk." Guide students as they skim the pages for math and nonmath vocabulary that may be unfamiliar or difficult to understand. Look at the pages with them and assess their understanding by asking, *Do you know what _____ means?* Have students raise their hands if they know the word's meaning. Create a list of words that need to be introduced or reviewed. Then have students take turns using multilingual glossaries and other translation tools to preteach the vocabulary to all students.

English Language Development Leveled Activities

Use the following problem with these leveled activities: For every four cats examined at the vet's office, there are five dogs examined. If the vet's office examines 92 cats in a week, how many dogs were examined the same week?

Entering/Emerging	Developing/Expanding	Bridging
Modeled Talk	**Report Back**	**Public Speaking**
Work as a group to solve the problem. As each step is completed, tell what you did, emphasizing correct pronunciation. Then have students repeat the key word. For example, say, *The **ratio** of cats to dogs is 4 to 5.* Then have students chorally repeat: **ratio**. Say, *I will write an **equation** to solve.* Have students chorally repeat: **equation**. Continue in this way, modeling pronunciation for each step in the solving process.	Ask pairs to work through the problem together. Number pairs 1 to 3, and assign a different number to each solving method (table, equation, or graph). Have pairs solve using their assigned method. Then have them report back to the class about how they solved their problem, using these sentence frames: **The unit rate is _____. We divided _____ by _____. We multiplied _____ by _____. We graphed the points _____ and _____. The constant of probability is _____. _____ dogs were examined.**	Have students work independently to solve the problem using any of the three methods: table, equation, or graph. Afterward, survey students to determine which methods they used. Organize students into small groups to discuss which method they used and why. Then ask volunteers to stand and express their opinions about which method was best for solving the problem. Remind them to speak clearly, politely, and look at the audience. Offer feedback about pronunciation, grammar, and the use of formal language.

Teacher Notes:

NAME _____ DATE _____ PERIOD _____

Lesson 6 Notetaking

Solve Problems Involving Proportional Relationships

Use the concept web to show three different ways to solve the proportional relationship problem.

Use a table.

Number of vans	1	3	9
Number of students	8	24	72

___Nine___ vans are needed.

Use an equation.

$y = kx$

$24 = k(3)$

$k = 8$

$72 = 8x$

$x = 72 \div 8$

$x = 9$

___Nine___ vans are needed.

A group of 24 students will ride in 3 vans to get to the zoo. If 72 students are going to the zoo, how many vans are needed? Assume the relationship is proportional.

Use a graph

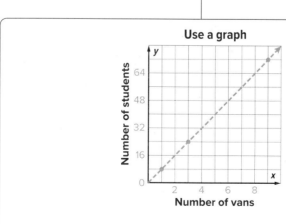

___Nine___ vans are needed.

6 **Module 1** *Proportional Relationships*

Lesson 1 Percent of Change

English Learner Instructional Strategy

Sensory Support: Mnemonics

Remind students that a percent of change can be an *increase* or *decrease*. Write *increase* and *decrease* on the board, then underline the *in* in *increase*. Tell students the *in-* prefix can mean "into." Model *into* by dropping pennies into a jar. Say, *I put pennies **into** the jar. I **add** pennies to the jar. This is an **increase**.* Write a plus sign next to *increase*. Then underline the *de* in *decrease* and tell students the *de-* prefix can mean "away." Model *away* by taking pennies out of the jar. Say, *I take pennies **away** from the jar. I **subtract** from the pennies in the jar. This is a **decrease**.* Write a minus sign next to *decrease*.

English Language Development Leveled Activities

Entering/Emerging	Developing/Expanding	Bridging
Word Knowledge Write and say: *compare*. Have students repeat. Coach them on forming the *r*-controlled vowel sound in the second syllable, which starts as /ā/ and glides into /r/. Then, make a T-chart with the headings Same and Different. Hold up two objects. Say, *Let's **compare**. Let's tell how they are the **same** and how they are **different**.* Discuss similarities. Say, *These are the **same**. Both [are/ have]* _____. List similarities under Same. Invite students' suggestions. Then discuss differences. Say, *These are **different**. One [is/has]* _____. List differences under Different.	**Share What You Know** <table><tr><td>Item</td><td>Cost in 2015</td></tr><tr><td>Gallon of milk</td><td>$3.31</td></tr><tr><td>Loaf of bread</td><td>$1.44</td></tr><tr><td>Gallon of gas</td><td>$2.40</td></tr></table> Display the table above, and discuss it with students. Then ask partners to use grocery store fliers or the Internet to find the price of each item today. Have them record the current price, as well as the price's percent of increase or decrease since the year 2015. Have pairs share their results with an emerging or bridging student.	**Building Oral Language** Have partners discuss what they know about percents of change. Have them share times in which they have experienced price increases or decreases, or times they have read about increases and decreases in things like sales, animal populations, and so on. Be sure that students identify whether the change was an increase or a decrease. Provide these sentence frames for students to use: **I experienced a percent of [increase/decrease] when** _____. **I read that there was a percent of [increase/decrease] in** _____ **because** _____.

Multicultural Teacher Tip

You may experience ELLs who appear to listen closely to your instructions and exhibit verbal and/or nonverbal confirmation that they understand the concepts. It may become clear during the lesson that they did not actually understand. This may be due to a student coming from a culture in which the teacher is regarded as a strong authority figure. They may be reluctant to ask questions, considering it impolite to do so and an implication that the teacher is failing.

Lesson 1 Vocabulary

Percent of Change

Use the vocabulary squares to write a definition, a sentence, and an example for each vocabulary word.

percent of change	Definition
	a ratio that compares the change in a quantity to the original amount
Example	Sentence
$\dfrac{2}{40} = 5\%$	A $40 sweater decreased in price by $2. The percent of change is 5%.

percent of increase	Definition
	a positive percent of change
Example	Sentence
$\dfrac{5}{10} = 50\%$	A $10 shirt had a price increase of $5. The percent of increase is 50%.

percent of decrease	Definition
	a negative percent of change
Example	Sentence
$\dfrac{15}{75} = 20\%$	A $75 jacket is on sale for $60. The percent of decrease is 20%.

Module 2 *Solve Percent Problems* **7**

Lesson 2 Tax

English Learner Instructional Strategy

Graphic Support: Word Webs

Write *Tax* in the middle of a word web. Discuss what students know about this word. Write down students' responses. Tell students that tax money is paid to the government, and the government uses the money to provide services to taxpayers. Tax is usually a percent of an amount of money, such as a price of a good.

Students will learn two types of tax in this lesson: income and sales tax. Add *sales tax* to an outer circle on the web. Ask students what they pay sales tax for. Write down their ideas. Be aware that some states do not charge sales tax and not all states charge sales tax for the same items. Add *income tax* to another circle on the outside of the web. Discuss what *income* is, and point out that the word is a compound word: *in/come*. Be aware that some states do not impose an income tax on residents. The vocabulary phrase *payroll tax* can be a sub-circle of *income tax*. It is the tax a company pays for all its employees.

English Language Development Leveled Activities

Entering/Emerging	Developing/Expanding	Bridging
Developing Oral Language Display the word web created in the ELL instructional strategy above. Say simple sentences about goods, services, and wages, such as *I am paid $10 per hour. What tax will I pay?* or *I will buy a new computer. What tax will I pay?* Have students tell whether you will pay a sales tax or an income tax. Review the frame: **You will pay [a sales/an income] tax.**	**Building Oral Language** Repeat the Entering/Emerging activity. Once students are clear on the differentiation between sales and income tax, have them use a sentence frame to practice conditional sentences. For example, **If you (are paid $10 per hour), you will (pay an income tax).**	**Make Cultural Connections** Have students ask their families about the taxes that are collected in their home countries. What type of taxes are collected? What goods and services are taxed? How much is sales tax? How much is income tax? Have students report their findings to the group.

Teacher Notes:

NAME _____ DATE _____ PERIOD _____

Lesson 2 Vocabulary

Tax

Use the definition map to write a list qualities about the vocabulary word or phrase. Sample answers are given.

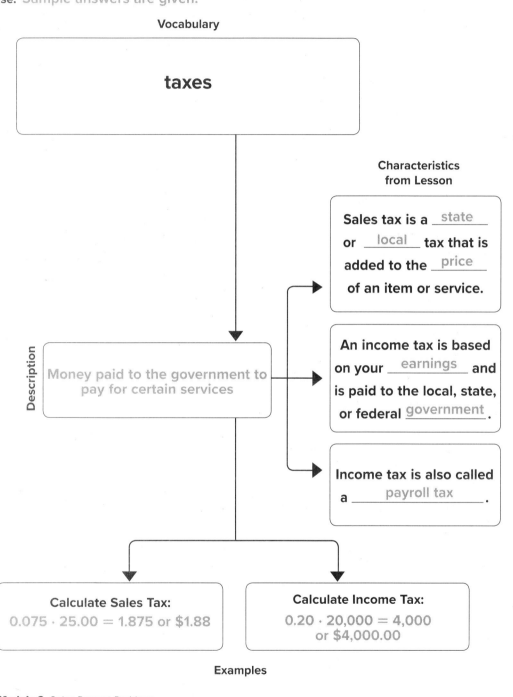

Vocabulary

taxes

Characteristics
from Lesson

Description

Money paid to the government to pay for certain services

Sales tax is a __state__ or __local__ tax that is added to the __price__ of an item or service.

An income tax is based on your __earnings__ and is paid to the local, state, or federal __government__.

Income tax is also called a __payroll tax__.

Calculate Sales Tax:
0.075 · 25.00 = 1.875 or $1.88

Calculate Income Tax:
0.20 · 20,000 = 4,000
or $4,000.00

Examples

Lesson 3 Tips and Markups

English Learner Instructional Strategy

Vocabulary Support: Frontload Academic Vocabulary

Review *selling price*. Preteach *wholesale cost, markup,* and *gratuity.* Write and say each term. Define *wholesale cost.* Explain that when the store buys an item from a supplier, they pay a *wholesale cost.* Ask, *Do you think the selling price is higher or lower than the wholesale cost?* **higher** Circle the word *up* in *markup.* Show how a *markup* is added to a wholesale cost and makes the price go *up.* The new price is the *selling price.*

To illustrate these concepts, draw a flowchart on the board that shows the process of how a store purchases a good from a supplier (for a wholesale cost), adds a markup, and then sells the good to a customer for a new selling price.

Then define *gratuity.* Explain that a *gratuity* (also called a *tip*) is a small amount of money paid for a service, in addition to what the service costs. Discuss reasons for paying a gratuity.

English Language Development Leveled Activities

Entering/Emerging	Developing/Expanding	Bridging
Word Knowledge	**Act It Out**	**Show What You Know**
Write *selling price, wholesale cost, markup,* and *gratuity.* Have students write each word on its own sticky note. As you give a clue about a word, have students hold up the correct sticky note(s). For example, if you say, *It is a percent,* students should hold up *gratuity* and *markup.* If you say, *What does the customer pay?,* students should hold up *selling price.* Continue with other examples to make sure students understand the meaning of each word. As they are able, introduce simple sentence frames, such as **A _____ is a percent. The _____ pays a _____.**	Review the concept of paying a *gratuity.* Then have students prepare a restaurant skit in groups of three. For each group, two students can play the part of a customer and one student can be the server. The server can leave a bill and say how much the total was. (**Here is your bill. The total amount is $20.00.**) The customers can discuss the quality of service to determine what percent gratuity they should leave. (**His service was great. I think we should leave a 20% gratuity.**) The server, after his customers leave, might say what the total gratuity was. (**Wow, they left me $4.00!**)	Organize students into pairs, and give them the following assignment: *1) Research and record the wholesale cost for three different items. 2) Write step-by-step instructions for adding a 20% markup on each item. 3) Show how to add sales tax to an item's selling price. Use a 7% sales tax rate.* Have partners compare and check their information with another pair.

Teacher Notes:

NAME _____ DATE _____ PERIOD _____

Lesson 3 Vocabulary

Tips and Markups

Use the three-column chart to organize the vocabulary in this lesson. Write the word in Spanish. Then write the correct terms to complete each definition.

English	Spanish	Definition
gratuity	gratificacíon	An additional amount of money paid in return for a ___service___. It is also called a ___tip___.
markup	margen de utilidad	The amount the ___price___ of an item is ___increased___ above the price the store paid for the item. selling price — ___wholesale cost___ = markup
selling price	precio de venta	The amount the customer ___pays___ for an item.
wholesale cost	el costo de venta por mayor	The amount a ___store___ pays for an item.

Module 2 *Solve Percent Problems*　**9**

Lesson 4 Discounts

English Learner Instructional Strategy

Vocabulary Support: Word Knowledge

Before the lesson, write *discount* on the board. Underline *count* and demonstrate its meaning. For example, say, *I will count my fingers.* Point to each finger as you count it, from one to ten. Then say, *I will count my students.* Gesture toward each student as you count him or her. Next, circle the letters *dis* in *discount*. Tell students that *dis-* is a prefix that means "opposite." Then explain that, within the context of this lesson, *discount* is a noun that means "an amount deducted from, or not counted in, the selling price." It is also a verb that means "to deduct from, or not count in, the selling price." It also has an adjective form, *discounted* (as in *discounted price*), that is used to describe items whose prices have been reduced, or lowered.

English Language Development Leveled Activities

Entering/Emerging	Developing/Expanding	Bridging
Signal Words and Phrases	Word Knowledge	Word Lists
Help students differentiate the phrases *for sale* and *on sale*. Write both phrases on the board, and have students say them with you. Then explain that items *for sale* are items to sell. Show students photos of different vendors selling goods. Point to a vendor and say, for example, *This person has food for sale. This person has art for sale.* Then explain that items *on sale* are sold at a discounted price. Show store ads with the word *Sale* on them. Point to items in the ads and say, for example, *This toaster is on sale. Its discount price is ____. This cereal is on sale. Its discount price is ____.*	Some students may confuse the terms *rate of discount, discount,* and *discount price*. Have students write each term on an index card. Then work as a class to define the terms using students' words. **Sample responses: *rate of discount*—a percent; *discount*—the amount of money the price is reduced; *discount price*—the cost after subtracting the discount.** Finally, encourage students to write notes and illustrations on their index cards, to help with remembering a term's definition. (Example: A synonym for *discount price* is *sale price*, because it is the price of an item *on sale*.)	Write: *sale price, selling price, discount, regular price, discount price, 40% off, markdown, discounted price, 40% discount* on the board. Have partners use these terms to create a synonyms word web. Show how to start by drawing a large circle and labeling it "Synonyms." Then demonstrate adding to the web by connecting other circles to the center circle. Tell students that each circle should contain two synonyms. Have partners compare their finished web with that of another pair of students. **sale price/discount price; selling price/regular price; discount/markdown; 40% off/40% discount**

Teacher Notes:

NAME _____ DATE _____ PERIOD _____

Lesson 4 Vocabulary
Discounts

Use the word cards to define each vocabulary word or phrase and give an example.

Word Cards

discount	**descuento**

Definition
the amount by which the
regular price of an item is
reduced

Definición
cantidad que se le rebaja al
precio regular de un artículo
_____

Example Sentence
A $40 sweater was marked down during the store's sale. The
discount was $5.

Word Cards

markdown	**rebaja**

Definition
an amount by which the
regular price of an item is
reduced

Definición
una cantidad por la cual el
precio regular de un artículo
se reduce

Example Sentence
A $40 sweater was marked down during the store's sale. The
markdown was $5.

Lesson 5 Interest

English Learner Instructional Strategy

Language Structure Support: Multiple-Meaning Words

Before the lesson, write *simple interest* and its Spanish cognate, *interés simple* on the Word Wall. Introduce the words, and provide math examples. Point out that both words within the term have multiple meanings. Use real-world objects, photos, and demonstrations to support understanding. Then write: *principal* on the board. Tell students that this is a multiple-meaning word, as well as a homophone for *principle.* Discuss how *principal* is more commonly used to refer to a person who is the head of a school. Show students the mnemonic, *A princi**pal** is a **pal** (friend)* to remind them that *principal* sometimes refers to a person. Then discuss its math meaning. Finally, explain that *principle* generally means "a rule or truth."

English Language Development Leveled Activities

Entering/Emerging	Developing/Expanding	Bridging
Word Knowledge	Partners Work/Pairs Share	Share What You Know
Demonstrate the meaning of *borrow.* Approach a student and say, *I **need** a math book.* Show that you don't have a math book. Then use gestures to communicate that you would like to use the student's book, while asking, *May I please **borrow** your math book?* When the student lets you have his or her book, say, *Thank you for letting me **borrow** your book.* Use the same procedure to request use of other classroom items, such as a pencil or paper. Then write: *take out a loan, buy on credit.* Use illustrations and role-playing to explain and show that these phrases name ways to borrow money.	Write and then read aloud this word problem: *Bryan borrows $6,000. His interest rate is 6.5% for 6 years. Dana borrows $5,000. Her interest rate is 8% for 6 years. Who will pay more interest? How much money will this person pay? Who will have to pay back more money in all? How much money will this person pay?* Have partners work together to solve the problem. Provide these sentence frames for forming responses: ____ **will pay more interest. [He/She] will pay $ ____. ____ will pay more money in all. [He/She] will pay a total of $____.** Then have partners compare answers with another pair.	Write and then read aloud this word problem: *Connor invests $2,500 at 3.5% for 4 years. Gabriela invests $4,000 at 2.5% for 3 years. Who will earn more interest on the money invested? How much money will he or she earn? Who will have more money at the end of the 3 or 4 year term? How much money will he or she earn?* Ask partners to work together to write step-by-step instructions for solving the problem. Then have them compare solutions with another pair of students. Once they are sure their answers are correct, have them explain their solutions to an emerging or expanding student.

Multicultural Teacher Tip

You may find ELLs write numbers using different notations. In the U.S., decimal numbers use decimal points (3.45), while other countries may use a comma (3,45). Greater numbers are separated into groups of three place values by commas in the U.S. (3,252,689), but in Latin American countries, the groups may be separated by points (3.252.689) or spaces (3 252 689). In Mexico, a combination of a comma and apostrophe (3'252,689) or a comma and semicolon (3;252,689) may be used.

NAME _____ DATE _____ PERIOD _____

Lesson 5 Vocabulary

Interest

Use the concept web to identify and describe the parts of the simple interest formula. Sample answers are given.

Word Bank			
simple interest	principal	annual interest rate	time

simple interest, the amount paid or earned for the use of money

principal, the amount of money deposited or borrowed

$$I = prt$$

annual interest rate, usually expressed as a percentage

time, expressed in years

Module 2 *Solve Percent Problems* **11**

Lesson 6 Commissions and Fees

English Learner Instructional Strategy

Vocabulary Support: Build Background Knowledge

Write the following on the board: *goods, services, price, fee, commission*. Helps students understand that a good is a thing, such as food, furniture, etc. and that a service is something done for a person. For example, a car is a good, and if someone washes your car for you, it is a service. Have students give other examples of goods and services.

Ask, *What is a price?* **the amount you pay for something** Tell students that goods have a price. Have students give examples of items that have a price. (e.g., milk, cars, books) Then say, *The price for a service is called a fee.* Say the word *fee* and have students repeat. Ask, *What do we pay a fee for?* **possible responses: school fees (tuition), ATM fee, parking fee** Tell students that one type of fee is called a commission. It is an amount of money paid to a salesperson. It is the percent of the price of the item the salesperson sold. People who sell cars and houses receive a commission.

English Language Development Leveled Activities

Entering/Emerging	Developing/Expanding	Bridging
Word Knowledge Have available several photos of goods and services (e.g., goods: toys, books, food, furniture; services: massage, doctor, dentist, lawn care service). Have students say **goods** or **services** for each photo you display.	**Developing Oral Language** Repeat the Entering/Emerging activity and have students use a sentence frame, such as, **A toy is a [good/service].** Then have students use another sentence frame to tell whether a price or a fee is paid for each one: **You pay a [price/fee] for a toy.**	**Turn & Talk** Review the different ways that people can be paid for their work, such as *hourly wage, salary, commission only, salary plus commission.* After introducing each method, have students turn and talk to another student about the pros and cons to that method of payment. After all methods have been introduced and discussed, have partners tell each other which way they would prefer to be paid and why.

Teacher Notes:

NAME _____ DATE _____ PERIOD _____

Lesson 6 Notetaking
Commission and Fees

Use Cornell notes to better understand the lesson's concepts. Complete each answer by filling in the blanks with the correct word or phrase.

Questions	Notes
1. What is a commission and how can I calculate it?	An employee sells ____goods____ or ____services____ for a company. The employee receives a commission. A ____commission____ is a payment equal to a ____percent____ of the amount of goods or services that an employee ____sells____. **Example** Carl sells a car for $25,000. His commission is 3%. His commission payment is $ ____750____.
2. What is a fee?	A fee is a ____payment____ for a service. A fee can be a ____fixed amount____, a ____percentage____ of the price, or ____both____. **Example** Marie bought a video game online for $50. The shipping fee was 10% of the cost of the game. The shipping fee was $ ____5.00____.
Summary	
How can I use the percent equation to find commissions and fees? See students' work.	

Lesson 7 Percent Error

English Learner Instructional Strategy

Language Structure Support: Tiered Questions

Write *percent* and its Spanish cognate, *por ciento,* on the board or a cognate chart. Review that *percent* means "for every 100" or "out of 100." Ask, *So, what is 20 percent?* If necessary, model and prompt students to say, **20 out of 100.** Repeat with several other examples.

Write *error.* Underline *err* and explain that the word means "to make a mistake." Write a few simple words or math equations on the board, including a few with spelling or calculation errors in them. For example, *persent, add, sudtract, multiply, devide,* $3 + 3 = 9, 3 \cdot 3 = 9.$
Ask questions according to students' level of English acquisition, such as:
Entering/Emerging: *Point to the error. Does this equation/word have an error?*
Developing/Expanding: *Which words have a spelling error?*
Bridging: *Find the errors and tell what the mistake is.*

Add *percent* and *error* to the Math Word Wall. Include visual examples.

English Language Development Leveled Activities

Entering/Emerging	Developing/Expanding	Bridging
Listen and Identify	**Round the Table**	**Share What You Know**
After introducing the concept, go over the steps for finding percent error one more time, perhaps writing the steps on the board. Review the steps by asking, *What do we find first?* **amount of error** *To find amount of error, do we add or subtract?* **subtract** Continue asking simple questions for which the answer is yes/no or a single word or phrase	Organize students in groups of four. Assign one student to be the "teacher." Give the group a percent error problem. Have the three "students" solve the problem with each student doing one step and the passing the paper to the next student to do the next step and so on. The "teacher" should be monitoring progress and offering assistance wherever needed.	Have partners create a "lesson plan" for teaching others how to find the percent error. First have them compile a list of information they must have (e.g., actual amount, estimate, amount of error) and prepare to introduce those concepts to others. Then have them prepare a numbered list of steps for finding the percent error. If time allows, have students partner with an Entering/Emerging or Developing/Expanding student and "teach" their lesson.

Teacher Notes:

NAME _____ DATE _____ PERIOD _____

Lesson 7 Vocabulary

Percent Error

Use the vocabulary squares to write a definition, a sentence, and an example for each vocabulary word.

	Definition
amount of error	the positive difference between the estimate and the actual amount
Example 43 years (actual age) − 38 years (estimate) = 5 years	**Sentence** Jesse guessed that Mr. Perez is 38 years old. Mr. Perez's actual age is 43. The amount of error is 5 years.

	Definition
percent of error	a ratio, written as a percent, that compares an amount of error (an estimate) to an actual amount
Example $\dfrac{\text{amount of error}}{\text{actual amount}} \cdot 100 = \dfrac{5}{38} \cdot 100$ $= 13.2\%$	**Sentence** The percent of error of Jesse's guess is 13.2%

Lesson 1 Add Integers

English Learner Instructional Strategy

Sensory Support: Physical Activities

On the board write *add* and *additive*. Point out the words' shared letters, and discuss how the words' meanings are related. Next, discuss *inverse*. Show students how inversing objects *turns* them into their opposites. For example, show students a hat. Say, *I will **turn** the hat to its **inverse** side*. Then turn the hat inside out and say, *Now the hat's **opposite** side shows*. Next, show students a coin that is heads side up. Say, *I will **turn** the coin to its **inverse** side*. Then turn the coin tails side up and say, *Now the coin's **opposite** side shows*. Then ask, *How do I form the additive inverse of a positive number?* Have students respond using this sentence frame: **Turn the positive number into a _____ number. (negative)**

After the lesson, add the terms *opposites* and *additive inverse* and their Spanish cognates, *opuestos* and *inverso aditivo*, respectively to a Word Wall with examples or drawings.

English Language Development Leveled Activities

Entering/Emerging	Developing/Expanding	Bridging
Act It Out	**Number Game**	**Show What You Know**
Have students work in pairs. Give each pair a set of positive and negative counters. Then write these expressions on the board: $5 + (-3)$; $-6 + 2$; $-3 + 7$; $4 + (-6)$; $-4 + 4$. One student should model the expression with the counters. The other student uses the sentence frame, **The sum is [positive/negative] _____.** to state the value of the expression. For the next expression, students switch roles. Remind students to remove all zero pairs from their models.	Divide students into pairs, and distribute 6 to 7 index cards to each pair. Have pairs write *opposites* on one card and *additive inverses* on another. Then have them write a different integer on each of their remaining cards. A player takes a turn by drawing one word card and one integer card. Then he or she uses the cards to form a sentence. For example, if the word *opposite* and the integer -3 are drawn, the player might say, **Negative three and positive three are opposites.** Students take turns drawing cards and making sentences until all their integer cards have been used.	Have students work with a partner to think of different ways the concept of *opposites* has been used in their math lessons and in real-world situations in which they use math. For example, in their lessons they have worked with *positive integers* and *negative integers*, and at home they may have *added* and *subtracted* money from their savings accounts. Have partners create a list of antonym pairs, based on their discussion. **Sample responses: working forward/working backward, multiply/divide, deposit/withdraw.** Then ask them to share their lists with the class.

Teacher Notes:

NAME _____ DATE _____ PERIOD _____

Lesson 1 Vocabulary

Add Integers

Use the word cards to define each vocabulary word or phrase and give an example. Sample answers are given.

Word Cards

opposites	opuestos

Definition

two integers that are the same

distance from zero, but on

opposite sides of zero

Definición

dos enteros que equidistant

de cero, pero en direcciones

opuestas

Example Sentence

The integers 2 and −2 are opposites; the sum of 2 and −2 is

zero.

Copyright © McGraw-Hill Education

Word Cards

additive inverse	inverso aditivo

Definition

two integers that are

opposites

Definición

dos enteros opuestos

Example Sentence

The additive inverse of 2 is −2. The additive inverse of −2 is 2.

Copyright © McGraw-Hill Education

Lesson 2 Subtract Integers

English Learner Instructional Strategy

Vocabulary Support: Frontload Academic Vocabulary

Before the lesson, review the meaning of these terms, which students will encounter in word problems: *platform, diving board, diver, surface; temperatures, moon, maximum, minimum, degrees, Celsius, balance, account, bank, charged, fee; sea, surface, range, elevation*. Use photos, realia, and demonstrations to help support understanding. Discuss how many of the words have multiple meanings, and point out the antonyms (*maximum/minimum*) and the word with a homophone (*sea/see*). Ensure students are familiar with the symbol for *degrees* and the abbreviation for *Celsius*. Finally, show students Alabama, Louisiana, New Mexico, California, and Florida on a map of the United States.

English Language Development Leveled Activities

Entering/Emerging	Developing/Expanding	Bridging
Build Background Knowledge	**Sentence Frames**	**Number Game**
Write the integers −3, 7, −8, −10, 9, 2 on the board. Point to the first and say, *This is negative three. What is the **opposite** of negative three?* **positive three** Invite a volunteer to come to the board and write: **3**. Continue in this manner until all the integers have been addressed. Next, write and say: 5 − (−1). Then say, *To subtract, I will add the **opposite**.* Write and say: 5 + 1 = 6. Continue by writing similar subtraction problems and having students tell you how to simplify them.	Write 5 − (−1) on the board. Read the problem aloud. Then say, *To subtract negative one from positive five, I will add positive one to positive five.* Write: 5 + 1. Then say, *Positive five plus positive one equals positive six.* Continue by writing other subtraction problems on the board and having students tell how to simplify them. Have students use these sentence frames to form their explanations: **To subtract ____ from ____, add ____ to ____. The answer is ____.**	Divide students into pairs, and give each pair two number cubes. Each partner rolls both cubes and then writes a subtraction problem using the two numbers rolled. Each number rolled may be used in the problem as a positive integer or a negative integer. Repeat this process three times. Partners then exchange papers and simplify the problems by changing them into addition problems. Partners check each other's answers.

Multicultural Teacher Tip

ELLs may use an alternative algorithm when solving subtraction problems. For example, Latin American students may have been taught the equal additions method of subtraction instead of the traditional U.S. method of "borrowing" from the column to the left when the top number is less than the bottom number.

In the equal additions method, a problem such as 35 − 18 solved vertically would start with ten ones added to the top number (15 − 8) and then one ten is added to the bottom number (30 − 20), to get 7 and 10, or 17. Similarly, 432 − 158 would be solved as 12 − 8, 130 − 60, and 400 − 200 (4 + 70 + 200 = 274).

NAME _____ DATE _____ PERIOD _____

Lesson 2 Notetaking
Subtract Integers

Use the flow chart to review the process for subtracting integers.
Sample answers are given.

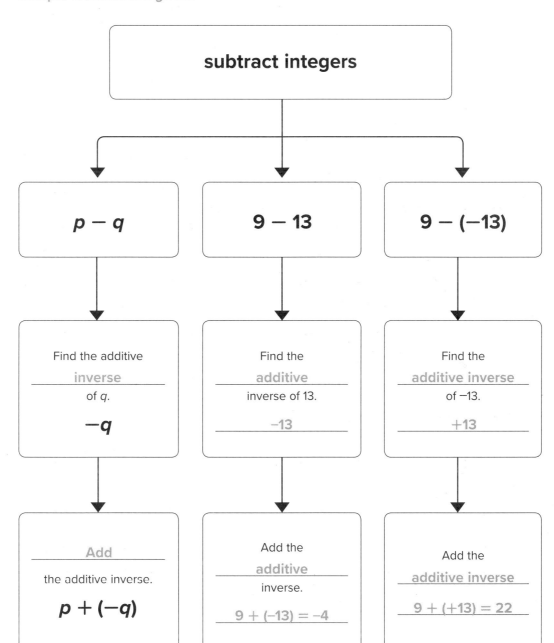

Lesson 3 Multiply Integers

English Learner Instructional Strategy

Vocabulary Support: Activate Prior Knowledge

Have students review the following statement and example: *The product of two numbers with different signs is negative.* $6(-4) = -24$. Point out that *parentheses* are used in place of a multiplication symbol to indicate that two numbers should be multiplied by each other. Show students how one integer is directly followed by another integer inside parentheses, with no spaces in between. Then say, *Let's rewrite a multiplication problem. How can I rewrite 2×-6 using parentheses?* Invite a volunteer to come to the board and rewrite the problem. **2(−6)**

English Language Development Leveled Activities

Entering/Emerging	Developing/Expanding	Bridging
Anchor Chart	**Listen and Identify**	**Number Game**
Write: 6×-7 on chart paper. Say, *This multiplication expression says "positive six times negative seven."* Point to the 6 and say, *This is a* **factor**. Have students repeat chorally as you label the 6 "factor." Point to the symbol and say, *This is the* **multiplication sign**. Have students repeat chorally as you label the symbol "multiplication sign." Point to the −7 and say, *This is a* **factor**. Have students repeat chorally as you label the −7 "factor." Then write: $6 \times -7 = 6(-7)$. Say, *Both expressions say the* **same** *thing.* Explain that in the second expression, no multiplication sign is needed because one *factor* in *parentheses* follows the other *factor*, with no spaces in between. Label the parts of the second expression.	Write 6×-7. Ask, *What kind of* **expression** *is this?* **a multiplication expression** *What are the* **factors**? **positive six and negative seven** Then say, *Now I will write this another way.* Write: $6(-7)$. Point to the symbols and say, *These are* **parentheses**. Discuss other ways parentheses are used in math, such as to group operations within a problem that has more than one operation. Write an example: $6 \times (1 - 8)$. Have students help you point out how the use of parentheses results in $6(-7)$.	Divide students into pairs, and give each pair a bag with 20 integer counters, 10 of each sign. Player 1 draws 10 counters from the bag and divides the counters into two groups. One group has negative signs, and the other group has positive signs. Each group represents a number, one positive and one negative. Player 1 multiplies the two numbers. Player 2 places all the counters back in the bag and draws 10 new counters. Player 2 multiplies the two numbers represented by the counters, as Player 1 did. Both players take four turns. Then each player adds the products from each of his or her turns. The player whose score is the *lowest* wins.

Teacher Notes:

NAME _____ DATE _____ PERIOD _____

Lesson 3 Notetaking
Multiply Integers

Use Cornell notes to better understand the lesson's concepts. Complete each sentence by filling in the blanks with the correct word or phrase.

Questions	Notes
1. What sign is the product of two integers with different signs?	The product of two integers with ___different___ signs is ___negative___ .
2. What sign is the product of two integers with the same sign?	The product of two integers with the ___same___ signs is ___positive___ .

Summary
When is the product of two or more integers a positive number? See students' work.

16   **Module 3** *Operations with Integers and Rational Numbers*

Lesson 4 Divide Integers

English Learner Instructional Strategy

Vocabulary Support: Activate Prior Knowledge

Before the lesson, remind students that addition and subtraction are related operations. Ask, *How are addition and subtraction related?* **They are opposites.** Then ask, *How is multiplication similar to addition?* **Multiplication is repeated addition.** Write: $(-4) + (-4) + (-4) = 3(-4)$. Discuss how adding -4 three times is like multiplying -4 by 3. Invite a volunteer to write the problem's solution: **−12.** Then say, *Like addition and subtraction, multiplication and division are opposites. If multiplication is repeated addition, what is division?* **repeated subtraction**

Finally, have students recall what they know about multiplying positive and negative integers. Ask, *When both factors have the same sign, is the product* **positive** *or* **negative***?* **positive** *When is the product negative?* **when the factors have different signs** Tell students to keep this in mind as they learn about dividing integers.

English Language Development Leveled Activities

Entering/Emerging	Developing/Expanding	Bridging
Listen and Identify Write: $-27 \div 3 = -9$. Say, *This is a* **division** *problem*. Then write and say: *dividend, divisor, quotient*. Point to -27 and say, *dividend*. Point to 3 and say, *divisor*. Point to -9 and say, *quotient*. Now write $-9 \times 3 = -27$. Say, *This is a multiplication problem.* Then point to the two problems you wrote and say, *These problems are* **related**. Point to -27 in the multiplication problem and say, *This is the product.* Then point to -27 in the division problem and ask, *What is -27 in the division problem?* **the dividend** Continue this process to help students relate 3 the *factor* to 3 the *divisor* and -9 the *factor* to -9 the *quotient*.	**Report Back** Divide students into pairs. Then write this problem on the board: $-12 \div 6 = -2$. Tell partners to write the problem on their own paper and then label each of its parts with one of these terms: *quotient, divisor, dividend*. Then ask them to write two multiplication problems that are related to the division problem. After students have had time to work, have them report their findings using these sentence frames: _____ **is the quotient.** _____ **is the divisor.** _____ **is the dividend.** Ask volunteers to write the two related multiplication problems on the board: **$-2 \times 6 = -12$, $6 \times (-2) = -12$**.	**Show What You Know** Write the following terms on the board: *factor, product, dividend, divisor, quotient*. Ask pairs of students to identify which terms apply to division and which apply to multiplication. Have partners write sentences telling how the multiplication terms relate to the division terms. For example: **The *product* of a multiplication problem becomes the *dividend* in a division problem.** Have students write a math example for each sentence, such as: **$-4 \times 3 = -12$; −12 is the product. $-12 \div 3 = -4$; −12 is the dividend.** Students can share their sentences and examples with the class.

Teacher Notes:

NAME _____ DATE _____ PERIOD _____

Lesson 4 Notetaking
Divide Integers

Use the flow chart to review the process for dividing integers. Sample answers are given.

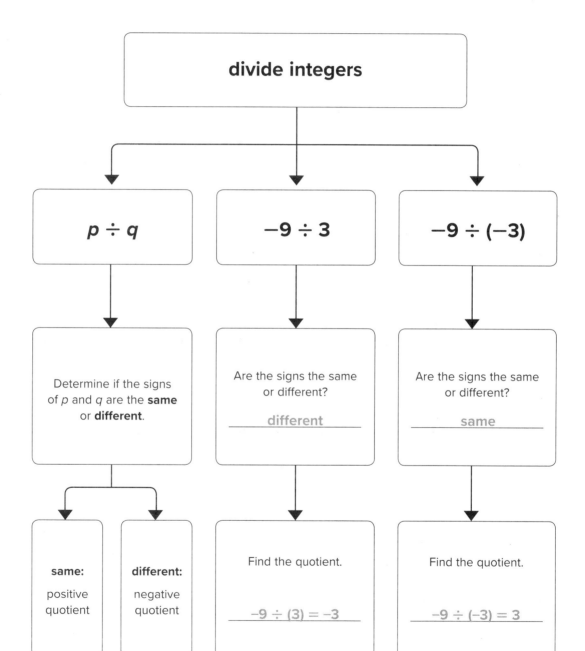

Lesson 5 Apply Integer Operations

English Learner Instructional Strategy

Sensory Support: Mnemonic Devices

Write *order of operations* on the board. Review the meaning of *order* and the mathematical meaning of *operations*. Ask students to list all the operations they can think of. Write their answers on the board. Introduce or review the correct order of operations and write them in a numbered list.

1) **P**arentheses or brackets (perform operations inside parentheses)
2) **E**xponents (evaluate the exponents)
3) **M**ultiply and **D**ivide (from left to right)
4) **A**dd and **S**ubtract (from left to right)

Point out that students can use the first letter of each (PEMDAS) to remember the correct order or operations. Have students add the order of operations to an anchor chart or word wall.

English Language Development Leveled Activities

Entering/Emerging	Developing/Expanding	Bridging
Look, Listen, and Identify Have students write each step in the order of operations on its own sticky note. Have students arrange the notes in order on their desks. Then have students check a partner's order to make sure it is correct. Discuss any differences. Teach the ordinal numbers *first, second, third,* and *fourth.* Introduce each word (and associate it with its corresponding cardinal number), say the word, and have students hold up the correct sticky note and repeat the word. Then ask, *What is the _____ step in the order of operations?* Students should hold up the corresponding sticky note.	**Signal Words and Phrases** Introduce or review words and phrases that signal order, such as *first, second, next, then, after that,* and *finally.* Have partners use the signal words or phrases in sentences that tell the correct order of operations. For example, they might write: **First, perform operations in parentheses. Then, evaluate the exponents. Next...** and so on. Ask volunteers to read their sentences to the group.	**Partners Work/Pairs Share** Have partners create a set of clues about order of operations. Encourage them to use words, phrases, and clauses that signal order. For example, **You do this after evaluating exponents from left to right. When you finish multiplying and dividing, you do this.** Have each pair trade clues with another pair who should use the clues to find the correct answer.

Teacher Notes:

NAME _____ DATE _____ PERIOD _____

Lesson 5 Review Vocabulary

Apply Integer Operations

Use the definition map to list qualities about the vocabulary word or phrase.
Sample answers are given.

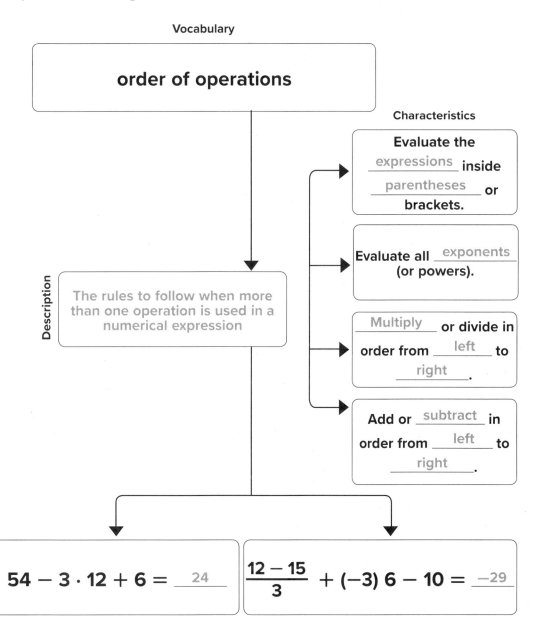

Vocabulary

order of operations

Characteristics

Evaluate the _expressions_ inside _parentheses_ or brackets.

Evaluate all _exponents_ (or powers).

Multiply or divide in order from _left_ to _right_ .

Add or _subtract_ in order from _left_ to _right_ .

Description

The rules to follow when more than one operation is used in a numerical expression

$$54 - 3 \cdot 12 + 6 = \underline{24}$$

$$\frac{12 - 15}{3} + (-3)\,6 - 10 = \underline{-29}$$

Simplify each expression.

Lesson 6 Rational Numbers

English Learner Instructional Strategy

Sensory Support: Pictures and Photographs

Before the lesson, write *bar notation* and its Spanish cognate, *notación de barra* on a Word Wall and provide math examples. Show the bar notation symbol alongside other bars, such as the bar graph, parallel bars used in gymnastics, and a granola bar. Have students tell how all the bars are alike. **Sample responses: All form straight lines, all are horizontal.** Then write: *note, notation.* Explain that one meaning of *note* is "to write something in a brief form." Discuss how symbols, abbreviations, words, and phrases take the place of complete words and sentences in notes. Then show/discuss how *note* and *notation* are related in meaning.

English Language Development Leveled Activities

Entering/Emerging	Developing/Expanding	Bridging
Exploring Language Structure	**Number Game**	**Developing Oral Language**
Write: *repeating decimal, terminating decimal.* Underline the *-ing* ending in *repeating* and *terminating,* and explain that this ending is sometimes added to a verb to make an adjective. Write and say, *A **repeating** decimal is a decimal that **repeats**. A **terminating** decimal is a decimal that **terminates**.* Underline *repeat* in *repeating* and *repeats* to show they share a base word. Do the same with *terminating* and *terminates.* Then write: *swinging door, running water, singing bird, sleeping baby.* Say each phrase with students. Then guide them to say its meaning: **A ____ing ____ is a ____ that ____s.**	Prepare several decks of 12 index cards. Each card in a deck shows a different fraction that is either positive or negative. Place students in groups of four. Give each group one deck. Discuss these game rules: 1) The object of the game is to order the cards from least to greatest. 2) Player 1 draws a card, writes the fraction as a decimal, and places it number side up. 3) Player 2 draws a card, writes the fraction as a decimal and places it to the left or right of Player 1's card, as appropriate. 4) Players continue drawing cards and placing them in a line until all cards are ordered correctly.	Have students work in pairs to create a three-column graphic organizer for the words *repeating, bar,* and *terminating.* The left column should list the words, the middle column should contain an everyday definition for each word, and the right column should contain the vocabulary word from this lesson and the mathematical definition for each word from the glossary. Afterward, discuss as a group how the everyday definitions for each word relate to the mathematical definitions.

Multicultural Teacher Tip

In some countries, students may learn to read and write from right-to-left. As they learn English, they may struggle with the switch to left-to-right. The difficulty may carry over into math, with a student attempting to write and solve problems backward.

NAME _____ DATE _____ PERIOD _____

Lesson 6 Vocabulary
Rational Numbers

Use the vocabulary squares to write a definition, a sentence, and an example for each vocabulary word. Sample answers are given.

repeating decimal	**Definition** the decimal form of a rational number
Example 0.1666..., 2.75000...., $-0.\overline{3}$	**Sentence** The decimal form of the fraction $\frac{1}{9}$ is a repeating decimal.

bar notation	**Definition** in repeating decimals, the line or bar placed over the digits that repeat
Example $2.\overline{63}$, $1.\overline{18}$, $0.\overline{32}$	**Sentence** In the number $2.\overline{63}$, the bar notation indicates that the digits 63 repeat.

terminating decimal	**Definition** a repeating decimal which has a repeating digit of 0
Example 0.25000..., 1.65, −0.825	**Sentence** Money values written in decimal form are terminating decimals.

Lesson 7 Add and Subtract Rational Numbers

English Learner Instructional Strategy

Vocabulary Support: Activate Prior Knowledge

Introduce the word *inverse*. Write $3 + 4 = 7$ on the board. Have students say the number sentence. Then repeat for $7 - 4 = 3$. Point out that the starting point was 3. Then 4 was added, and then subtracted, to end up at the starting point again. Tell students that the word *inverse* means "opposite." Addition and subtraction are inverse operations.

Write the following on the board: *sum, difference, positive, negative, absolute value, number line*. Introduce or review the words. Then draw a number line on the board and have volunteers give examples of each term by drawing them on the line or explaining them using the number line. Have them plot $+\frac{1}{2}$ and $-\frac{1}{2}$ on the number line.

Point out how $+\frac{1}{2}$ and $-\frac{1}{2}$ are additive inverses. Write *additive inverse* on the board, say the word, and have students repeat. Underline *add* and point out that when additive inverses are added together, the sum is zero. Have students give other examples of additive inverses.

English Language Development Leveled Activities

Entering/Emerging	Developing/Expanding	Bridging
Word Knowledge Write opposite on the board. Give a few simple examples of opposites, such as *happy/sad or bright/dark*. Have students give other examples. Then challenge students to give examples of number that are opposites. If they need assistance, write −3 on the board or on a number line. Ask, *What is the opposite?* Guide students to the idea that the number on the opposite side of zero that is the same distance from zero is the opposite. Write opposite *numbers = additive inverses*. Say the term and have students repeat.	**Developing Oral Language** Have partners ask and answer questions using sentence frames, such as **What is the additive inverse of ____? The additive inverse of ____ is ____. What is the opposite of ____? The opposite of ____ is ____. Give an example of additive inverses. ____ and ____ are additive inverses.**	**Share What You Know** Have students work with Emerging partners on the concept of additive inverses. Mentors should focus on making sure their partners understand the meaning of the term and the language for expressing their knowledge. Encourage mentors to offer sentence frames as students are able.

Teacher Notes:

NAME _____ DATE _____ PERIOD _____

Lesson 7 Vocabulary

Add and Subtract Rational Numbers

Use the concept web to write pairs of rational numbers written in different forms and in the same form. Sample answers are given.

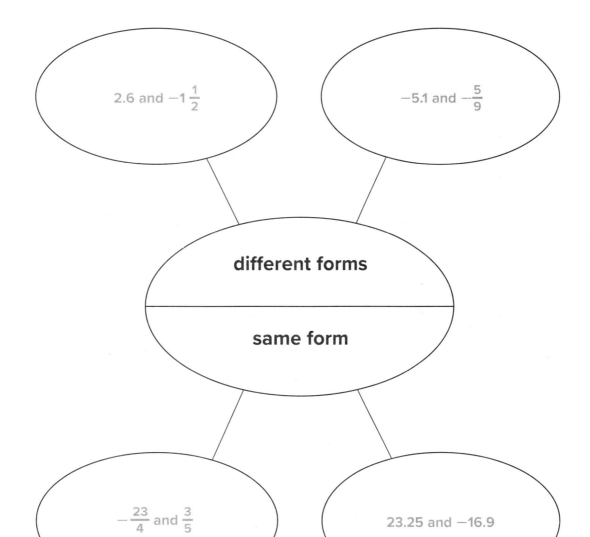

2.6 and $-1\frac{1}{2}$

-5.1 and $-\frac{5}{9}$

different forms

same form

$-\frac{23}{4}$ and $\frac{3}{5}$

23.25 and -16.9

Lesson 8 Multiply and Divide Rational Numbers

English Learner Instructional Strategy

Collaborative Support: Partners Work/Pairs Check

Have partners work on problems you assign. Pair emerging students with expanding/bridging students. Have one partner complete the first problem while the second acts as coach. Then have partners switch roles for the second problem. When they have finished the second problem, have them get together with another pair to check answers. When both pairs have agreed on the answers, have them continue working in their original pairs on the next two problems. For more complicated problems, ask the more fluent partner to help with interpreting and setting up the problem, and have the less fluent partner solve. After all problems have been completed, have students come together as a class to discuss answers.

English Language Development Leveled Activities

Entering/Emerging	Developing/Expanding	Bridging
Word Knowledge	**Report Back**	**Number Game**
Write: *reciprocal.* Help with its pronunciation: Show that the *c* is followed by an *i*, which makes the *c* say /s/, instead of /k/. Then demonstrate that the *i* makes a short sound, not a long sound. Have students say the word with you. Next, write: $\frac{1}{3}, \frac{3}{14}, \frac{5}{2}, \frac{6}{11}$, and $\frac{8}{9}$. Show students the reciprocal of $\frac{1}{3}$. Say, *The **reciprocal** of $\frac{1}{3}$ is its **reverse**: $\frac{3}{1}$.* Do the same for $\frac{3}{14}$. Then help students tell the reciprocal of each remaining number, using this sentence frame: _____ **is the reciprocal of** _____.	Write the following expressions on the board: $\frac{1}{3} \div \frac{3}{14}, \frac{5}{2} \div \frac{6}{11}, \frac{8}{9} \div \frac{5}{2}, \frac{8}{9} \div \frac{2}{13}$. Point to each fraction and have students say it with you. Have students rewrite each expression as a multiplication expression, simplify it, and write the answer in simplest form. Check responses for the class. Have all students stand. Then ask one student to tell the answer to a problem, and have him or her sit down, along with any other students who have the same response. Continue until all students are seated. Then work through the problem as a class.	Divide students into pairs, and give each pair a deck of number cards. Discuss these game rules: 1) Choose three cards. Make a mixed number using the three cards. Choose three more cards and make another mixed number. 2) Work with your partner to divide the numbers. Record all the steps and the quotient. 3) Take turns choosing cards, forming mixed numbers, and dividing mixed numbers. After several rounds, have them explain their method for dividing mixed numbers to an developing/expanding student.

Multicultural Teacher Tip

As students begin simplifying fraction division problems, you may notice some ELLs are not multiplying by the reciprocal of the divisor. In Mexico and Latin America, students are commonly taught to cross multiply when dividing fractions. The numerator of the first number is multiplied by the denominator of the second number to find the numerator of the answer, and vice versa for the denominator of the answer. For example, $\frac{1}{3} \div \frac{3}{4}$ is solved as $\frac{1 \times 4}{3 \times 3}$ to get $\frac{4}{9}$.

NAME _____ DATE _____ PERIOD _____

Lesson 8 Notetaking

Multiply and Divide Rational Numbers

Use Cornell notes to better understand the lesson's concepts. Complete each sentence by filling in the blanks with the correct word or phrase.

Questions	Notes
1. How do I multiply fractions?	_____Multiply_____ the numerators and the _____denominators_____. Then simplify.
2. How do I divide fractions?	_____Multiply_____ by its multiplicative inverse, or _____reciprocal_____ .
3. How do I divide mixed numbers?	First, I rename the mixed number as a fraction greater than one, or an _____improper_____ fraction. Then I multiply the first fraction, by the _____reciprocal_____ of the second fraction.

Summary

How is dividing fractions related to multiplying fractions? See students' work.

_____

_____

_____

_____

_____

_____

_____

_____

Module 3 *Operations with Integers and Rational Numbers* **21**

Lesson 9 Apply Rational Number Operations

English Learner Instructional Strategy

Language Structure Support: Cognates

Write the following words and their cognates on the board: *order of operations (orden de las operaciones, Commutative Property (propiedad commutativa), Associative Property (propiedad asociativa),* and *simplify (simplificar).* Introduce or review each term.

Then write an expression and have partners use order of operations to simplify it. You might use: $\frac{1}{2}\left(2 + \frac{3}{3}\right) - \frac{5}{8}$. Once they are finished, ask questions to clarify that students understand the lesson vocabulary presented here. For example, *What is the first step?* **perform the operation in parentheses** Remind students to simplify their answer.

Point out cognates for math vocabulary whenever possible and have students add the words to an anchor chart or word wall.

English Language Development Leveled Activities

Entering/Emerging	Developing/Expanding	Bridging
Listen and Identify Review the order of operations using the PEMDAS mnemonic device. Write an expression on the board, such as $\frac{1}{2}\left(2 + \frac{3}{4}\right) - \frac{5}{8}$. Ask, *What do we do first (next, after that, etc.)?* Allow one-word responses, such as **parentheses.** Say, *Yes, we add the numbers in parentheses.* Continue asking questions to guide students to simplify the expression.	**Show What You Know** Assign one of the following words to each student: *order of operations, Commutative Property, Associative Property, simplify.* Have them create their own definition of the word and then prepare a short presentation giving an example of the term. Encourage the audience to ask questions to the presenter. Once each presentation is complete, lead a short discussion to answer the question, *Why is [term] important?*	**Communication Guides** Have students write the steps for simplifying the expression $\frac{1}{2}\left(2 + \frac{3}{4}\right) - \frac{5}{8}$. Then have them adjust their set of directions to include a few "mistakes." When they are done, have students trade with another student who should then review the list and make corrections. To encourage conversational language, write a few suggestions students can use to express themselves, such as, **Uh oh, I think I found a mistake. I don't think this one is correct. Should you ____ before doing this step? Let's go through this step together.**

Teacher Notes:

NAME _____ DATE _____ PERIOD _____

Lesson 9 Review Vocabulary

Apply Rational Number Operations

Use the three-column chart to organize the vocabulary and key words in this lesson. Write the word in Spanish. Then complete the definition of each word.

English	Spanish	Definition
order of operations	orden de las operaciones	The _____rules_____ to follow when more than one _____operation_____ is used in a numerical expression
Associative Property	propiedad asociativa	The way in which numbers are grouped does not change the _____sum_____ or _____product_____ .
Commutative Property	propiedad commutativa	The _____order_____ in which two numbers are _____added_____ or _____multiplied_____ does not change the sum or product.
simplify	simplificar	Write an expression in simplest form

Lesson 1 Powers and Exponents

English Learner Instructional Strategy

Language Structure Support: Tiered Questions

Add *base* and *exponent* and their Spanish cognates, *base* and *exponente,* on a Word Wall with examples or drawings to support understanding. Provide an exponent and have students recall what they learned in previous grades.

During the lesson, be sure to ask questions according to each student's level of English comprehension. Ask emerging level students simple questions that elicit one-word answers or allow the student to respond with a gesture: *Which number is the power? Is this the base?* or *Do I use _____ as a factor _____ times or _____ times?* For expanding students, ask questions that elicit answers in the form of simple phrases or short sentences: *How do I know which number to multiply? What do I need to do first?* or *Which numbers are the exponents?* For bridging students, ask questions that require more complex answers: *Why is _____ used as a factor _____ times?*

English Language Development Leveled Activities

Entering/Emerging	Developing/Expanding	Bridging
Academic Vocabulary	**Act It Out**	**Developing Oral Language**
Guide students to create a classroom anchor chart with visual examples and labels for *power, base,* and *exponent.* As you provide an example for each word and identify it, have students chorally repeat the vocabulary word. Monitor correct pronunciation and repeat the modeling as needed. In particular, listen to how students are saying *power,* as the /ow/ sound is not used in Spanish and may give students difficulty.	Divide students into small groups of three or four. Distribute a pair of number cubes to each group. Say, *Roll your number cubes to create a power. Use the greater number as the base and the lesser number as the exponent. Write the power and find its product.* Give students time to complete the task. Then have the students in each group take turns describing the power using the following sentence frames: **The base is _____. The exponent is _____. The power is _____. The product of the power is _____.**	Have students work in pairs to create a three-column graphic organizer for the words *power, base,* and *exponent.* The left column should list the words, the middle column should contain an everyday definition for each word, and the right column should contain the mathematical definition for each word from the glossary. Afterward, discuss as a group how the everyday definitions for each word relate to the mathematical definitions.

Teacher Notes:

NAME _____ DATE _____ PERIOD _____

Lesson 1 Vocabulary

Powers and Exponents

Use the word bank to identify the parts of the expression. Draw an arrow from the word to the part of the expression it describes. Then use the three-column chart to organize the vocabulary. Write the word in Spanish. Then write the definition of each word. Sample answers are given.

Word Bank			
power	base	exponent	factor

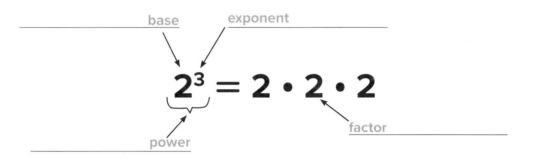

English	Spanish	Definition
power	potencia	product of repeated factors with an exponent and a base
base	base	in a power, the number that is the common factor
exponent	exponente	in a power, the number of times the base is used as a factor

Lesson 2 Multiply and Divide Monomials

English Learner Instructional Strategy

Graphic Support: K-W-L Chart

Write *monomial* and its Spanish cognate, *monomio*, on the Word Wall. Provide a concrete example by writing $3 \cdot 3 \cdot 3 \cdot 3 = 3^4$ or 81 and then identifying each monomial in the equation.

Display a K-W-L chart. In the first column, record what students learned in the previous lesson about powers. In the second column, record what students hope to learn during the lesson, including the use of the Laws of Exponents to simplify expressions that have multiple powers. After the lesson, display the following sentence frame and have students use it to describe what they learned during the lesson: **I learned that _____.** Use the third column of the K-W-L chart to record student responses.

English Language Development Leveled Activities

Entering/Emerging	Developing/Expanding	Bridging
Look, Listen, and Identify	Report Back	Listen and Write
Write $6^4 \cdot 6^2$ and say, *We can simplify this expression.* As you model simplifying, ask questions that students can answer as a group with thumbs up for **yes** or thumbs down for **no**. For example, point to the base of one power and ask, *Is this the exponent?* **no** Or ask, *Do I add the exponents?* **yes** Other questions you might ask are: *Do we add the bases? Do we multiply the exponents? Are the bases the same?* and so on. Repeat the activity by simplifying $\frac{8^5}{8^3}$.	Have students work in pairs. Randomly assign one problem to each pair. Give pairs time to work together to solve their assigned problems. Display the following sentence frames: **We were [multiplying/dividing] powers, so we [added/subtracted] the exponents. The expression _____ simplified is _____.** Have pairs use the sentence frames, share their answers, and describe how they simplified the expressions.	Group students into pairs. Write $x^4y^3z \cdot x^2z$ while one partner in each pair copies the expression on a sheet of paper. Addressing the other partners, say *Tell your partner how to simplify this expression.* Have these students explain each step as the students with the papers follow along to simplify the expression. Afterward, have pairs exchange papers to check each other's work. Write another expression with powers that can be simplified, and have the students switch roles as they repeat the activity.

Multicultural Teacher Tip

Students from some countries will not refer to *billion* as a place value until there are at least 13 digits. Instead, they refer to *thousand millions*, and *billion* is introduced when U.S. students would refer to *trillions*. For example, a U.S. student would read the number 564,321,000,000 as "five hundred sixty-four *billion*, three hundred twenty-one *million*," whereas a Latin American student would read it as "five hundred sixty-four *thousand*, three hundred twenty-one *million*."

NAME _____ DATE _____ PERIOD _____

Lesson 2 Vocabulary

Multiply and Divide Monomials

Use the definition map to list qualities about the vocabulary word or phrase. Sample answers are given.

Vocabulary

monomial

Characteristics: What it is.

can be a number

Description

a number, variable, or product of a number and one or more variables

can be a variable

can be a product of a number and one or more variables

 15^2 $x + 6$ $2y^2 - 3z$ $4ac$

Circle the expressions that are monomials

Lesson 3 Powers of Monomials

English Learner Instructional Strategy

Graphic Support: Venn Diagram

Display a Venn diagram. Label one side *Power of a Power* and the other side *Product of Powers*. Provide an example of each, such as $(6^4)^2$, $5^2 \cdot 5^3$, and a combination of the two $(6^4)^2 \cdot 6^8$. Then ask students to compare and contrast how each is simplified. Display the following sentence frames for students to use as they compare similarities and differences: **The bases are _____. The exponents are _____. When you simplify, you _____ the exponents.** Record student answers in the appropriate areas of the diagram.

As students work on practice problems, allow emerging students to partner with expanding or bridging students who share their native language. Have the emerging student participate in the discussion by suggesting answers to his or her partner using their native language. Then have the more proficient English speaker translate the answer to English.

English Language Development Leveled Activities

Entering/Emerging	Developing/Expanding	Bridging
Look, Listen, and Identify	**Numbered Heads Together**	**Building Oral Language**
Write $(4z^4)^2$ and say, *We can simplify this expression.* As you model simplifying the expression, have students guide you by answering questions that can be answered with a single word. For example, point to the base and ask, *Do I add or multiply the exponents 4 and 2?* **multiply** Other questions you might ask are: *Will the base become 8 or 16?* **16** *Is z a base or an exponent?* **base** Provide another power of a power that can be simplified and repeat the activity.	Have students get into groups of four. Ask the students in each group to number off as $1-4$. Have the students in each group work together to find the volume of a cube with a side length of $3w^4$. Display the following sentence frames: **The formula for the volume of a cube is _____. The length of one side is _____. The expression _____ can be used to find the volume. The expression _____ simplified is _____.** Choose numbers from 1–4 to designate which student in each group will use the sentence frames to describe their group's answer.	Have students get into six groups, and then assign one problem to each group. Say, *First, write the expression, then simplify the expression, and last, write out the expression in standard form.* Give groups time to complete the task. Afterward, compare the three versions and discuss why it is beneficial to have more than one way to write an expression.

Teacher Notes:

NAME _____ DATE _____ PERIOD _____

Lesson 3 Notetaking

Powers of Monomials

Use Cornell notes to better understand the lesson's concepts. Complete each sentence by filling in the blanks with the correct word or phrase.

Questions	Notes
1. How do I find the power of a power?	I can _____multiply_____ the _____exponents_____ .
2. How do I find the power of a product?	I can find the _____power_____ of each _____factor_____ and _____multiply_____ .

Summary
How does the Product of Powers law apply to finding the power of a power?
See students' work.
_____
_____
_____
_____
_____
_____

Module 4 *Exponents and Scientific Notation* **25**

Lesson 4 Zero and Negative Exponents
English Learner Instructional Strategy

Vocabulary Support: Utilize Resources

As students review and utilize previously-taught vocabulary, such as *numerator, denominator, exponents,* and *powers of ten,* be sure to remind them that they can refer to a glossary or dictionary for help. Direct students to other translation tools as well if they are having difficulty with non-math language in the word problems.

Pair emerging level students with more proficient English speakers. Display the following sentence frames: **If the exponent is zero and the base is not zero, then _____. If the exponent is positive, then _____. If the exponent is negative, then _____.** Say, *Use the sentence frames to write three rules about powers.* Have the students in each pair complete the sentence frames. Then have the pair share what they have written.

English Language Development Leveled Activities

Entering/Emerging	Developing/Expanding	Bridging
Word Recognition	**Think-Pair-Share**	**Report Back**
Before the lesson, create a set of index cards with *add, subtract, multiply,* and *divide* written on them. Randomly distribute the cards so each student has one. As you work through problems from the lesson, have students guide you by prompting them with either/or questions for each step, such as *Do I add or subtract these numbers?* or *Do I multiply the exponents or add them?* Have students with the correct cards hold them up, and then choose one of these students to come forward and complete that step with you.	Before the lesson, use index cards to create matching pairs of expressions with positive and negative exponents, such as $10^3 \cdot 10^{-6}$ and $\frac{1}{10^3}$ or $y^{-2} \cdot y^{-3}$ and $\frac{1}{y^5}$. Distribute one card to each student. Say, *Find the student with a card showing an equivalent expression.* Give students time to find their partners. Then say, *Explain why the expressions are equivalent.* Display the following sentence frame for students to use when sharing their explanations: **_____ and _____ are equivalent because _____.**	Assign a problem to each student. Say, *Rewrite the problem using multiplication or division, and then simplify the expression.* Give students time to complete the task. Then display the following sentence frames for students to use in reporting back on how they arrived at an answer: **I rewrote _____ as _____. I [added/ subtracted] the exponents. I simplified _____ to _____.** Have students evaluate each others' work and make suggestions when an incorrect answer is shared.

Multicultural Teacher Tip

In Mexico and Latin American countries, negative numbers can be represented two different ways: with either a negative sign in front of the number (i.e. −3) or with a horizontal line directly above the number (i.e. $\overline{3}$). The latter approach may be confusing, as it is also the common format for representing repeating decimals.

NAME _____ DATE _____ PERIOD _____

Lesson 4 Review Vocabulary
Zero and Negative Exponents

Use the definition map to list qualities about the vocabulary word or phrase. Sample answers are given.

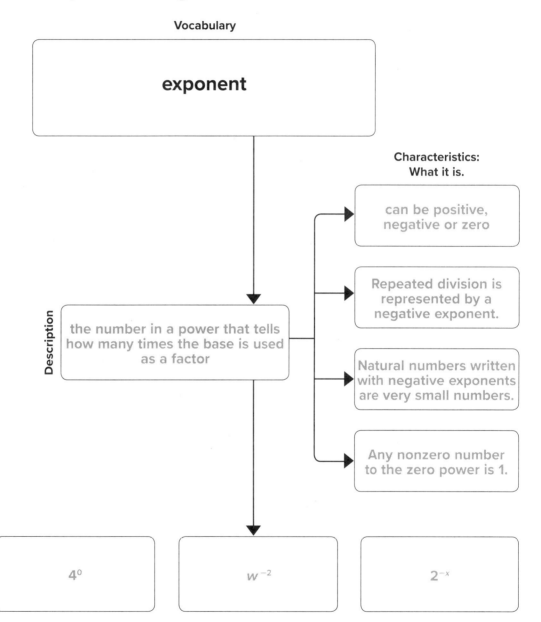

Vocabulary

exponent

Description: the number in a power that tells how many times the base is used as a factor

**Characteristics:
What it is.**

can be positive, negative or zero

Repeated division is represented by a negative exponent.

Natural numbers written with negative exponents are very small numbers.

Any nonzero number to the zero power is 1.

4^0

w^{-2}

2^{-x}

Write examples of terms that contain a negative or zero exponent.

26 **Module 4** *Exponents and Scientific Notation*

Lesson 5 Scientific Notation

English Learner Instructional Strategy

Collaborative Support: Pass the Pen

Write the word *scientific notation* and its Spanish cognate, *notación cientifica,* on the Word Wall. Provide a concrete example by displaying a science text or other resource that includes numbers written using scientific notation.

After the lesson, divide students into small groups. Be sure each group contains students of varying levels of English proficiency. Have the students in each group take turns completing the steps necessary to solve their assigned problem. As they work, have each student write a sentence on a strip of paper describing his or her step. Provide the following sentence frames:

Using scientific notation, ____. I moved the decimal point to the ____. The number is [greater than/less than] 1, so the exponent is [positive/negative].

English Language Development Leveled Activities

Entering/Emerging	Developing/Expanding	Bridging
Memory Device Write 3.23×10^{-6}. Circle *6* and point to the negative sign as you ask, *Is this on the left or the right of six?* Give students a chance to answer. Then say, *The negative sign is on the left. We move the decimal left. How many places do we move the decimal left?* **6** Model moving the decimal and adding zeros. **0.00000323** Divide students in half so there is one group on the left and one on the right. Write additional examples of scientific notation. Have students on the left help with negative exponents and those on the right with positive exponents.	**Listen and Write** Distribute number cubes to student pairs. Write 6.54×10 and say, *Roll your number cube to create an exponent for 10.* Then assign each pair to have either a positive or a negative exponent. Have one student in each pair write the expression, including the positive or negative exponent, on an index card. Then say, *Tell your partner how to rewrite the expression in standard form.* Provide the following sentence frame: **Move the decimal ____ places to the ____.** Write a new expression and have students switch roles.	**Turn and Talk** Ask, *How is scientific notation useful in the real world?* Have students turn to the student nearest them to briefly discuss the answer. Then lead a discussion about the usefulness of scientific notation versus standard form. Display a sentence frame to help students during the discussion: **Scientific notation is useful because ____.** Ask students to think of examples when writing numbers using standard form would be inconvenient and record their answers.

Teacher Notes:

NAME _____ DATE _____ PERIOD _____

Lesson 5 Vocabulary
Scientific Notation

Use the vocabulary squares to write a definition, a sentence, and a description for each vocabulary word. Sample answers are given.

	Definition
powers of 10	ten raised to any power
Example	**When would you use this?**
$10^2, 10^{-5}, 10^1, 10^{-3}$	when using scientific notation

	Definition
standard form of a number	the usual way of writing a number that shows place values
Example	**When would you use this?**
25,000	writing numbers in everyday life

	Definition
scientific notation	a compact way of writing numbers with absolute values that are very large or very small
Example	**When would you use this?**
2.5×10^4	in a science experiment

Lesson 6 Compute with Scientific Notation

English Learner Instructional Strategy

Language Structure Support: Sentence Frames

During the lesson, provide sentence frames such as the following to aid students in participating in the practice exercises:

Entering/Emerging: **Move the decimal _____ places. The power of ten is _____.**

Developing/Expanding: **Move the decimal _____ places to the _____. The exponent changes to _____.**

Bridging: **_____ must be rewritten as _____ because _____. The decimal must be moved _____ because _____.**

Have students work in small groups. Assign one problem to each group that they will solve together. Afterward, have a volunteer use the sentence frames to report back on how his or her group found the answer.

English Language Development Leveled Activities

Use the following problem with these leveled activities: *Evaluate each expression. Express the result in scientific notation.* $(3.9 \times 10^2)(2.3 \times 10^6) = $ _____

Entering/Emerging	Developing/Expanding	Bridging
Word Knowledge	Building Oral Language	Exploring Language Structures
Invite four students forward and assign them as *first, second, third,* and *fourth*. Write the problem on the board and then, to the right, write *First*. Say, *First we need to multiply the decimal numbers.* Say, *first* again, have students repeat chorally. Then have the student assigned as *first* perform the task. Then write *Second* and repeat the activity for the next step. Continue in this manner for steps three and four. Choose a new problem and repeat the activity with four new students.	Divide students into several small groups to symplify the problem. Display the following sentence frames: **First _____. Next _____. Then _____. Last _____.** Say, *Use the sentence frames to record each step as you symplify.* Give groups time to simplify the problem. Then ask a volunteer from each group to read the steps they took to simplify the problem.	As you model simplifying the problem, write out each step using complete sentences, such as *1. I rewrite _____ as _____. 2. I multiply _____ and _____.* and so on. Afterward, write another nearly identical problem for students to simplify on their own. Then say, *Use the sentences I've written to describe how you simplified the problem, but use the past-tense.* Listen for correct usage of the past tense and remodel as necessary.

Teacher Notes:

NAME _____ DATE _____ PERIOD _____

Lesson 6 Notetaking
Compute with Scientific Notation

Use Cornell notes to better understand the lesson's concepts. Complete each sentence by filling in the blanks with the correct word or phrase.

Questions	Notes
1. How do I multiply and divide with scientific notation?	I can _____multiply_____ the _____factors_____ and use the Product of Powers to _____add_____ the _____exponents_____ . I can _____divide_____ the _____factors_____ and use the Quotient of Powers to _____subtract_____ the _____exponents_____ .
2. How do I add and subtract with scientific notation?	First, I line up the _____place values_____ and rewrite each expression with the same power of _____10_____ . Then, I use the Distributive Property and add or subtract the _____factors_____ . Finally, I _____rewrite_____ in scientific notation.

Summary

How does scientific notation make it easier to perform computations with very large or very small numbers? See students' work.

_____

_____

_____

_____

_____

_____

_____

Lesson 1 Roots

English Learner Instructional Strategy

Collaborative Support: Peers/Mentors

Write *radical sign* and its Spanish cognate, *signo radical*, on the Word Wall. Draw an example of a radical sign and use it as you discuss what students have learned in previous grades about squares and square roots.

Divide students into small groups with students of varying levels of English proficiency. As students work the first few problems, ask expanding or bridging students to answer first, and then encourage emerging students to repeat the answer in English. When emerging students are confident, invite them to be the first to answer their problems. Encourage them to use the sentence frame:

The square root of _____ **is** _____.

English Language Development Leveled Activities

Entering/Emerging	Developing/Expanding	Bridging
Multiple Word Meanings Draw a 5-by-5 array. Say, *This shows five times five or 25. What is the shape?* Give students a chance to answer, **square**. Then say, Yes. *It is a square. Five rows and five columns make 25.* Write $5 \cdot 5 = 25$ and $\sqrt{25} = 5$. Say, *Five squared is 25. So, five is the* **square root** *of 25.* Say, *square root* again as you point to the the square root symbol and have students repeat chorally.	**Frontload Academic Vocabulary** Divide students into five groups and assign each group one of the lesson vocabulary words: *square root, perfect square, cube root, perfect cube,* and *radical sign*. Have students list on an index card one or two everyday definitions for the individual words that make up each compound (*square, root, sign,* and so on). Have students flip the card over and write the math definition for each vocabulary word. Then have groups present both the math and non-math definitions and discuss how they are related.	**Developing Oral Language** Divide students into small groups and assign each group one of the following perfect squares: 9, 16, 25, 49, 64, 81. Say, *Write a real-world story problem that uses your assigned number and its square root.* If students need help getting started, you might suggest problems involving area or square arrays of seating, plantings, and so on. Give groups time to complete the task, and then have them present their story problems to the other students.

Teacher Notes:

NAME _____ DATE _____ PERIOD _____

Lesson 1 Vocabulary
Roots

Use the three-column chart to organize the vocabulary in this lesson. Write the word in Spanish. Then write the definition of each word. Sample answers are given.

English	Spanish	Definition
square root	raíz cuadrada	one of two equal factors multiplied to form perfect squares
perfect square	cuadrados perfectos	a rational number whose square root is a whole number
radical sign	signo radical	the symbol used to indicate a non-negative square root, $\sqrt{\ }$
cube root	raíz cúbica	one of three equal factors of a number
perfect cube	cubo perfectos	rational number whose cube root is a whole number

Module 5 *Real Numbers* **29**

Lesson 2 Real Numbers
English Learner Instructional Strategy

Vocabulary Support: Cognates

Write *irrational number* and its Spanish cognate, *número irracional,* on the Word Wall with examples or drawings to support understanding. During the lesson, frequently refer to them to reinforce meaning and provide concrete examples of each word.

Write the prefix *ir-* and say, *This word part means "not." When it is added to the beginning of a word, it changes the word's meaning.* Remind students that *irrational* means "not rational," and then have them brainstorm other examples of words that use the *ir-* prefix, such as *irregular, irreversible, irresistible,* and *irresponsible.* Point out that *ir-* has the same meaning in English as in Spanish.

Refer students to a glossary or dictionary if they need a review of definitions for the different real number types: *natural numbers, whole numbers, integers,* and *rational numbers.*

English Language Development Leveled Activities

Entering/Emerging	Developing/Expanding	Bridging
Word Recognition Create a set of index cards so each student will have a card. On each card, write one of the following real number types: *natural, whole, integer, rational, irrational, real.* Distribute one card to each student. One at a time, display a wide variety of different number types and help students identify which number sets each falls into. For example, write 13.6 and say, *13.6 is a rational number. It is a real number.* Have students with either of those cards stand and say the word on their card. Be sure each number set is used multiple times.	**Partners Work** Write: *Order the set* { $\sqrt{5}$, *220%, 2.25, 2.$\overline{2}$} from least to greatest.* Have students work in pairs to complete the exercise. Then discuss what steps had to be taken first before some numbers could be located on the number line. Display a sentence frame to help students: **First we had to** _____. Then have students identify which set or sets each number as originally written belongs to. Display another sentence frame to help students: _____ **is a** _____.	**Verbal/Linguistic Learners** Have students work in pairs. Provide each pair with a list of five number types: *natural, whole, integer, rational, irrational.* Tell students to take turns giving their partners numbers and asking the partner to categorize each number according to the list of number sets. The student who provides a number should then state whether he or she agrees or disagrees with the partner's categorization and why. Challenge students to find a wide enough variety of numbers so that all sets are included.

Multicultural Teacher Tip

ELLs who are familiar with the U.S. standard for placing the angle symbol at the front of a number or angle designation may be confused by the use of inequality symbols. They may have trouble distinguishing between the two signs, so it is important to emphasize the difference prior to beginning the lesson.

NAME _____ DATE _____ PERIOD _____

Lesson 2 Vocabulary
Real Numbers

Use the word cards to define each vocabulary word or phrase and give an example. Sample answers are given.

Word Cards

irrational number

Definition

a number that cannot be written as the quotient $\frac{a}{b}$, where a and b are integers and $b \neq 0$

Example Sentence

The square root of 2 is an irrational number.

números irracionales

Definición

número que no se puede expresar como el cociente $\frac{a}{b}$, donde a y b son enteros y $b \neq 0$

Word Cards

real numbers

Definition

the set of rational numbers together with the set of irrational numbers

Example Sentence

The set of real numbers include integers, fractions, mixed numbers, percents, and irrational numbers.

número real

Definición

el conjunto de númerous racionales junto con el conjunto de númerous irracionales

Lesson 3 Estimate Irrational Numbers

English Learner Instructional Strategy

Language Structure Support: Choral Responses

As you work through the lesson and narrate the steps taken to estimate roots and cube roots, have students chorally repeat math words and phrases after you have said them. Prompt students by saying the math word or phrase a second time, emphasizing the correct pronunciation. Then have students chorally respond by repeating the word or phrase back to you. Listen closely for errors in pronunciation and model a second time if necessary.

Remember that some common sounds used in English may be unfamiliar to ELLs. For example, the /o͞o/ sound in *root* and the /kw/ sound in *square* are not used in some other languages. Students may also have difficulty with plurals, differentiating between /s/ at the end of *roots* and /z/ at the end of *squares* and *cubes*.

English Language Development Leveled Activities

Entering/Emerging	Developing/Expanding	Bridging
Listen and Identify	**Show What You Know**	**Round the Table**
List a few perfect and non-perfect squares. Point to each as you ask, *Perfect or not perfect?* Ask a volunteer to answer. Then say the answer: *perfect* or *not perfect*. Have students repeat chorally. Choose a non-perfect square and model estimating its square root by plotting it on a number line ranging between two perfect squares. Point to each end of the line as you ask, *Is the square root of _____ closer to _____ or _____?* Display the following sentence frame to help students answer: **The square root of _____ is closest to _____.** Repeat with a non-perfect cube.	Display a Word Web with *-er* written in the center and another one with *-est*. Have students brainstorm examples of comparatives and superlatives that use each ending and record them. Pair students and assign the following: $\sqrt{35}$ and $\sqrt[3]{62}$ to each pair. Display the following sentence frames to help them share their answers: **The greatest perfect square/cube less than _____ is _____. The least perfect square/ cube greater than _____ is _____. _____ is closer to _____, so the best estimate is _____.**	Write: The number of swings back and forth of a pendulum of length L in inches per minute is $\frac{375}{\sqrt{L}}$. About how many swings will a 40-inch pendulum make each minute? Divide students into groups of three, and assign one problem to each group. Have students work jointly on the problem by passing the paper around the table to complete each step. Direct each member of the group to write with a different color to ensure all students participate. Afterward, have groups share their answers, and have the students in each group describe the specific steps they completed.

Teacher Notes:

NAME _____ DATE _____ PERIOD _____

Lesson 3 Notetaking
Estimate Irrational Numbers

Use Cornell notes to better understand the lesson's concepts. Complete each sentence by filling in the blanks with the correct word or phrase.

Questions	Notes
1. How do I estimate a square root?	First, I determine if the square root is a perfect _____square_____ . If not, then I use a _____number line_____ to determine between which two perfect _____squares_____ the square root falls and estimate based on where the square root falls on the number line.
2. How do I estimate a cube root?	First, I determine if the cube root is a perfect _____cube_____ . If not, then I use a _____number line_____ to determine between which two perfect _____cubes_____ the cube root falls and estimate based on where the cube root falls on the number line.

Summary

How can I estimate the square root of a non-perfect square? See students' work.

_____

_____

_____

_____

_____

_____

_____

Module 5 *Real Numbers* **31**

Lesson 4 Compare and Order Real Numbers
English Learner Instructional Strategy

Graphic Support: Number Lines

Review the vocabulary and language for the following types of numbers: *whole numbers, natural numbers, fractions, decimals, rational numbers, irrational numbers, real numbers integers.* Have students give examples of each type of number. Write their ideas on the board.

Draw a number line. Then tell students that they are going to put the example numbers in order on the number line. Ask, *How can we do this?* Students might say, **Compare numbers.** or **Find the smallest number first**. Suggest that students put all of the numbers in the same notation; for example, make all the numbers in decimal form, if possible. (Some numbers will have to be estimated.) Then have them put the numbers (estimates) on the number line.

Finally, have students use available language to compare two values at a time.

English Language Development Leveled Activities

Entering/Emerging	Developing/Expanding	Bridging
Choral Responses	Sentence Frames	Communication Guides
Have students compare two numbers on the number line. Say, *Point to the smaller number.* Students point. Model the sentence _____ **is the smaller number.** Have students repeat chorally. Then ask (about the same two numbers), *Is _____ greater than _____?* Model _____ *is greater than _____*. Have students repeat chorally. When students are firm as a group, have a few students say a sentence individually.	Assign a few numbers to each pair of students. Have them use any of the following sentence frames to compare the numbers and order them. _____ **is [greater/less] than _____. _____ is [bigger/smaller] than _____. _____ is the [greatest/ least] number. _____ is [first/ second/ next/last/and so on] in order.**	Have partners repeat the Developing/Expanding activity. Then extend the activity to include more advanced language by using the following frames: _____ **is [greater/less/bigger/smaller] than _____, so it is [first/second/ next/ last/and so on] in order. Because _____ is [greater/less] than _____, it goes [first/second/...] in order. The [first/second/next/...] number is _____ because it is [greater/ less] than _____.**

Teacher Notes:

NAME _____ DATE _____ PERIOD _____

Lesson 4 Vocabulary
Compare and Order Real Numbers

Use the three-column chart to organize the vocabulary and key words in this lesson. Write the word in Spanish. Then complete the definition of each word.

English	Spanish	Definition
repeating decimal	decimal periódico	Decimal form of a ___rational___ number
terminating decimal	decimal finito	A repeating decimal where the repeating digit is ___zero___
square root	raíz cuadrada	One of the two ___equal___ factors of a number. If $a^2 = b$, then ___a___ is the square root of ___b___.
rational number	número racional	A number that can be written as the ___ratio___ of two ___integers___ in which the denominator is not ___zero___. All integers, fractions, mixed numbers, and percents are rational numbers.
irrational number	números irracionales	A number that cannot be expressed as the quotient $\frac{a}{b}$, where a and b are ___integers___ and $b \neq$ ___0___.
real numbers	número reales	The set of ___rational___ numbers together with the set of ___irrational___ numbers.

Lesson 1 Simplify Algebraic Expressions

English Learner Instructional Strategy

Vocabulary Support: Multiple-Meaning Words

Before the lesson, write *constant* and its Spanish cognate, *constant*. Introduce the words, and provide math examples. Utilize other translation tools for non-Spanish speaking ELLs. Add the words to a Word Wall. Then discuss noun and adjective meanings for the word, using real-world objects and demonstrations to support understanding.

Then write: *term*. Have students recall the meaning of *term*. **Each number in a sequence is a term.** Then say, *In math, a **term** can also be a **part** of an algebraic expression.* Tell students that terms do not contain addition or subtraction signs; they only contain numbers and/or variables and multiplication or division.

English Language Development Leveled Activities

Entering/Emerging	Developing/Expanding	Bridging
Word Knowledge	**Developing Oral Language**	**Share What You Know**
Show how this lesson's vocabulary words are related using a word web. In the center circle, write: *term*. Say it with students, and help students to define it using their own words. Then around the center circle draw three smaller circles. In each, write one of the following words: *constant, coefficient, like terms*. Say each word with students. Connect its circle to the center circle to show that it is related to a term. Then invite volunteers to write examples of a constant, a coefficient, and like terms in the appropriate circle. Finally, help students define each word. Encourage students to use the word web as a reference.	Have students recall what *like fractions* are. **fractions with the same denominator** Then divide students into pairs. Have partners compare and contrast *like fractions* and *like terms*. Provide these sentence frames for them to use during their discussion: *Like fractions* and *like terms* are similar because _____. *Like fractions* and *like terms* are different because like fractions have _____ and like terms have _____.	Have Bridging students mentor Entering/Emerging and Developing/Expanding students on translating words into algebraic expressions, and vice versa, as follows: 1) Have each student write an algebraic expression. Then have them trade expressions and translate them into words. (Example: **4x + 13 says, "Four times the variable x plus thirteen."**) Have the more fluent students help with translation and correct pronunciation as needed. 2) After completing several turns, the pairs should work backward, translating verbal expressions into algebraic expressions.

Teacher Notes:

NAME _____ DATE _____ PERIOD _____

Lesson 1 Vocabulary

Simplify Algebraic Expressions

Use the vocabulary squares to write a definition, a sentence, and an example for each vocabulary word. Sample answers are given.

term	**Definition** a number, a variable, or a product or quotient of numbers and variables
Example $\frac{1}{5}$, $3x$, 2, $\frac{y}{7}$	**Sentence** $5x$ and 3 are both terms in the expression $5x - 3$.

like terms	**Definition** terms that contain the same variables raised to the same power
Example $3x$ and $9x$, y^2 and $7y^2$	**Sentence** The terms $6a$ and $2a$ are like terms.

constant	**Definition** a term that does not contain a variable
Example 5, 7, 15	**Sentence** In the expression $3x + 5$, the constant is 5.

Lesson 2 Add Linear Expressions
English Learner Instructional Strategy

Sensory Support: Illustrations, Diagrams, Drawings

Before the lesson, write *linear expression* and its Spanish cognate, *expresión lineal*. Introduce the words, and provide math examples. Utilize other translation tools for non-Spanish speaking ELLs. Add the terms to a Word Wall. Then write: *line/linear*. Underline *line* in both words, and tell students that *line* is the base word of *linear*. Then circle the *ar* in *linear* and tell students that this suffix means "resembling, or like." Help students create a definition for *linear* using its base word and suffix meaning. **resembling, or like, a line** Then draw a straight line, and discuss ways an expression might be like a line. Help students to think figuratively, guiding them to see that a line is *simple* and *direct*, as compared to shapes and squiggles.

English Language Development Leveled Activities

Entering/Emerging	Developing/Expanding	Bridging
Word Knowledge	Listen and Write	Turn and Talk
To help students understand how to add linear expressions, use the concept of perimeter. Write and say the word *perimeter*. Then explain its meaning, "the distance around a shape's outer edge." Use a pointer to show the perimeters of classroom objects. Trace their outer edges and say, *This is the* **perimeter** *of the* ____. Next, briefly discuss how to measure the perimeter of an object. Then draw simple shapes, give measurements using a variable for their sides, and have students find their perimeter measurements. Have students say the measurements, using this sentence frame: **The perimeter is** ____ **inches.**	Repeat the Entering/Emerging Level activity. Then have partners create their own linear expression problem about the perimeter of a triangle. Discuss the following guidelines: *1) Draw a triangle. 2) Label the triangle with a measurement for each of its sides. Each measurement must include at least one term and one x variable.* After partners have drawn and labeled their shape, have them exchange papers with another pair and find the perimeter of the shape they received.	Ask students to turn and talk to a neighbor about ways that a linear expression is like a line. After students have had a few minutes to discuss, have them share their ideas with the class. Finally, have students discuss why the expression $x - 7$ is linear but the expression $x^4 - 7$ is not.

Teacher Notes:

NAME _____ DATE _____ PERIOD _____

Lesson 2 Vocabulary

Add Linear Expressions

Use the definition map to list qualities about the vocabulary word or phrase.
Sample answers are given.

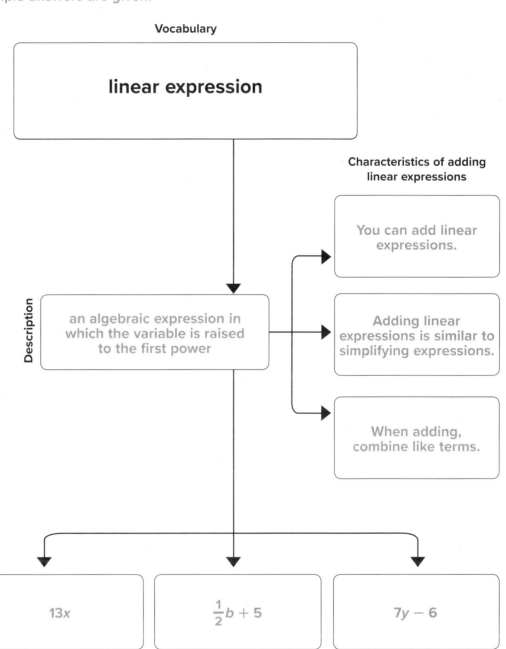

Vocabulary

linear expression

Description

an algebraic expression in which the variable is raised to the first power

Characteristics of adding linear expressions

You can add linear expressions.

Adding linear expressions is similar to simplifying expressions.

When adding, combine like terms.

$13x$

$\frac{1}{2}b + 5$

$7y - 6$

Examples of linear expressions

34 **Module 6** *Algebraic Expressions*

Lesson 3 Subtract Linear Expressions

English Learner Instructional Strategy

Vocabulary Support: Activate Prior Knowledge

Before the lesson, have students recall what they have learned about linear expressions. Write this on the board: $(-2x - 6) + (3x + 5) = $ _____. Then have students guide you through these steps toward its solution: 1) Use the Distributive Property. 2) Simplify. 3) Arrange the terms in columns of like terms. 4) Add like terms. After the class has solved the problem, have students tell you how to rework it using algebra tiles.

Then write: *additive inverse.* Remind students that they learned about additive inverses. Ask, *What is the **inverse** of something?* **its opposite** Then write these numbers: $-3, 2, 5, -6$. Have students tell each number's additive inverse. As needed, remind them that when a number is added to its additive inverse, the sum is zero.

English Language Development Leveled Activities

Use the following problem with these leveled activities: *The number of customers in a store on the first day is represented by $(6x - 3)$. The number of customers on the second day is represented by $(x - 1)$. Write an expression to find how many more customers visited the store on the first day. Then evaluate the expression if x is equal to 50.*

Entering/Emerging	Developing/Expanding	Bridging
Modeled Talk	**Report Back**	**Partners Work/Pairs Check**
Work as a group to solve the problem. As each step is completed, tell what you did, emphasizing correct pronunciation, then have students repeat the key word. For example, say, *The **linear expression** is $(6x - 3) - (x - 1)$.* Then have students chorally repeat: **linear expression**. Say, *The **additive inverse** of $(x - 1)$ is $(-x + 1)$.* Then have students chorally repeat: **additive inverse**. Continue in this way, modeling pronunciation for each step in the solving process.	Ask pairs to work through the problem together. Then have them report back to the class about how they solved their problem, using these sentence frames: **The linear expression is _____. The additive inverse of _____ is _____. If *x* equals 50, the there were _____ more customers on the first day.** Have the class check their solution to the problem.	Have partners work together to complete the problem. After they have solved it, have them write a couple sentences telling how they arrived at the solution. Then have them check answers with another pair of students. Students should use the sentences they wrote to justify their answer.

Teacher Notes:

NAME _____ DATE _____ PERIOD _____

Lesson 3 Notetaking

Subtract Linear Expressions

Use Cornell notes to better understand the lesson's concepts. Complete each sentence by filling in the blanks with the correct word or phrase.

Questions	Notes
1. How do I subtract linear expressions?	I subtract _____ like _____ terms. I use _____ zero _____ pairs if needed.
2. What is the additive inverse of a linear expression?	The additive inverse of a linear expression is an expression with terms that are _____ opposites _____. The sum of a linear expression and its additive inverse is _____ zero _____.

Summary
How can I use the additive inverse to help you subtract linear expressions? See students' work. _____ _____ _____ _____ _____ _____

Module 6 *Algebraic Expressions* **35**

Lesson 4 Factor Linear Expressions
English Learner Instructional Strategy

Vocabulary Support: Build Background Knowledge

Write *monomial* and *factored form* and their Spanish cognates, *monomio* and *forma factorizada,* respectively on a Word Wall. Introduce the words, and provide math examples to support understanding. Underline *mono* in *monomial,* and explain this root word means "one." Write a few examples of monomials and non-monomials on the board for visual support. Point out that the "Monomial" examples have only *one* term each, while the "Not Monomial" examples have two or more terms. Discuss other words with this root, such as *monotone, monologue,* and *monopoly.*

English Language Development Leveled Activities

Entering/Emerging	Developing/Expanding	Bridging
Word Knowledge	**Anchor Chart**	**Partners Work/Pairs Check**
Write: $2 \cdot 2 \cdot 5 = 20$ and *factored form.* Underline *factor.* Point to 2 and ask, *Is 2 a factor?* **yes** Repeat with 5. Help students define *factor.* Then circle the *ed* in *factored.* Explain that sometimes the *-ed* ending is used to make a noun into an adjective, which is a describing word. Show and explain how *factored* describes *form*: The *factored form* of an expression is the *form* that shows its *factors.* Finally, write expressions in both their factored and unfactored forms. Ask, *Which is the factored form?* Students point to the answer.	Draw a four-column chart on the board, with these column heads: Factor (noun), Factor (verb), Factored Form, Greatest Common Factor. Then, under each head, have students help you write the following: 1) a math definition for the term, using students' words; 2) a sentence that uses the term in context; and 3) a math example. The following are sample responses for the noun *factor*: **1) Definition: a number or variable multiplied by another number or variable to form a product; 2) One factor of 21 is 7; 3) Factors of 21 are 1, 3, 7, 21.**	Have partners work together to write word problems involving monomials. Tell them their word problems must include information that can be represented in a linear expression and a solution that involves factoring the expression. Then have students trade their problems with another pair and solve the word problem they receive. Finally, have partners check answers with the pair who wrote the problem.

Multicultural Teacher Tip

You may see some ELLs using a method other than the factor trees commonly used in U.S. classrooms to find factors. In Mexico, students are taught to draw a vertical line. On the left side, they write the number to be factored, and then the first prime factor is written on the right side. The number divided by the factor is then written on the left side, below the original number. The next factor is written on the right, and the process continues until there are no more factors. In factoring 18, for example, the result would be *18, 9, 3, 1* listed on the left side, and the prime factors *2, 3, 3* listed on the right.

18	2
9	3
3	3
1	

NAME _____ DATE _____ PERIOD _____

Lesson 4 Vocabulary
Factor Linear Expressions

Use the vocabulary squares to write a definition, a sentence, and an example for each vocabulary word. Sample answers are given.

monomial	Definition a number, variable, or product of a number and one or more variables
Example $13x$, -9, 27, y	Sentence A monomial contains only one term.

factor (verb)	Definition to write an expression as a product of its factors
Example $3x = 3 \cdot x$	Sentence We can factor the expression $10b$ as $10 \cdot b$.

factored form	Definition an expression written as the product of its factors
Example $27b + 3c = 3(9b + c)$	Sentence The factored form of $5y + 10$ is $5(y + 2)$.

Lesson 5 Combine Operations with Linear Expressions

English Learner Instructional Strategy

Vocabulary Support: Math Word Wall

Create a class word wall to review all the vocabulary in this module. Assign one or two of the following words to each pair of students: *terms, like terms, coefficient, constant, simplest form, linear expression, additive inverse, factor, factored form greatest common factor, monomial, distributive property, and simplify*. Have them work together to write the word, its cognate (if applicable), a definition, and an example. Before adding the information to the word wall, ask a volunteer from each pair to present the information to the class. Clear up any mistakes or misunderstandings (either with language or with the math content), and then have students add the information to the wall.

English Language Development Leveled Activities

Entering/Emerging	Developing/Expanding	Bridging
Look, Listen, and Identify Review the following terms and write them on the board: *combine like terms, factored form, distributive property*. Write a linear expression, such as $4(5 - x) - x$. Point to the expression and ask, *What is this?* **linear expression** Say, *We are going to simplify this expression.* Have students use one of the terms to answer your questions: *What do we do first?* **distributive property** *What do we do next?* **combine like terms** Repeat for other expressions.	**Signal Words and Phrases** Write a linear expression, such as $4(5 - x) - x$. Introduce or review words and phrases that signal order, such as *first, second, next, then, after that,* and *finally*. Have partners discuss how to simplify the expression and then use the signal words or phrases in sentences that tell the correct order for simplifying the expression.	**Building Oral Language** Review how to produce complex sentences. Remind students that a complex sentence has one independent clause (which can stand alone as a sentence) and at least one dependent clause (which cannot stand alone). Select one construction, write a sentence frame for it, and have students practice it. For example, **After you have _____, you should _____.** (Remind students that a verb with *-ed* will fill the first blank.) Other possibilities include: **Once you are finished _____ing, _____. Before you _____, you should _____.**

Teacher Notes:

NAME _____ DATE _____ PERIOD _____

Lesson 5 Review Vocabulary

Combine Operations with Linear Expressions

Complete the four-square chart to review the multiple-meaning word or phrase.
Sample answers are given.

Everyday Use	Math use in a sentence
to make something easier to understand or easier to do The Internet has helped simplify the research process.	The expression $3x + 5y + (-2y) - 5(2x)$ simplifies to $-7x + 3y$.

simplify

Math Use	Example from this lesson
to write an expression in a simpler way by combining like terms and eliminating parentheses Simplify the expression $3x + 5y + (-2y) - 5(2x)$.	Simplify $-2(x + 3) + 8x$. $-2(x + 3) + 8x = -2x - 6 + 8x$ $= 6x - 6$

Lesson 1 Write and Solve Two-Step Equations: $px + q = r$

English Learner Instructional Strategy

Language Structure Support: Communication Guides

Review the terms *add, subtract, multiply, divide, equation, coefficient, constant*, and *variable*. Ask volunteers to define each term, offering an example as support. Prior to beginning the lesson, scan through the lesson to find any vocabulary students might be unfamiliar with and preteach it. When students come upon a word you have taught ahead of time, they may not remember its meaning, but they will likely remember having already heard the word. The more exposure they have ahead of time, the easier it will be when students encounter difficult words, and the more likely students will be to ask for help.

Help students with language that they can use when they need to request help. For example, **Excuse me. May I ask a question? I have a question. I wonder about _____. What is a _____? Is this a _____? I am confused. What is the difference between _____ and _____? I can't remember what _____ means. Can you help me?**

English Language Development Leveled Activities

Entering/Emerging	Developing/Expanding	Bridging
Look, Listen, and Identify Write a story problem on the board and read it with students. For each word in the problem, point to it and ask, *Is this an important word?* When students say **yes**, write down the word. Then use the important words in a sentence that tells what is known. Then use simple words and phrases to guide students to define the variable and write the equation.	**Think-Pair-Share** Write a story problem on the board or direct students to a problem or example from the module. Ask students to read the problem and identify and list only the most important words. Then have them define the variable and write the equation. Finally, have students turn to another student and compare results. Ask volunteers to share with the group. Tell students that the words and variables might be slightly different, but the equation should be the same.	**Exploring Language Structure** Review the language for commands. Have students follow your directions as you give commands, such as *Stand up. Raise your hand. Sit down. Smile.* Write an example on the board. Ask, *Is this a complete sentence?* Students might say **no** because there does not appear to be a subject. Tell them that since these are commands, the implied subject is *You.* Have students use this information to write the steps for writing and solving a two-step equation as though they were giving commands to another person. Then have them say the commands to a partner who should follow them.

Teacher Notes:

NAME _____ DATE _____ PERIOD _____

Lesson 1 Vocabulary

Write and Solve Two-Step Equations: px + q = r

Use the definition map to list qualities about the vocabulary word or phrase.
Sample answers are given.

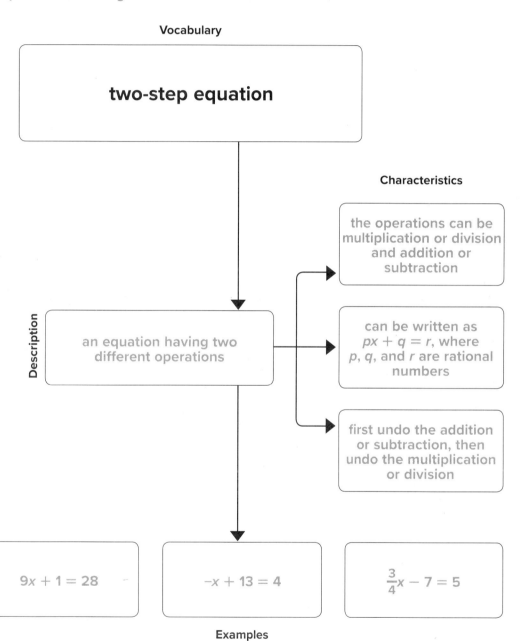

Vocabulary

two-step equation

Characteristics

the operations can be multiplication or division and addition or subtraction

Description

an equation having two different operations

can be written as $px + q = r$, where p, q, and r are rational numbers

first undo the addition or subtraction, then undo the multiplication or division

$9x + 1 = 28$

$-x + 13 = 4$

$\frac{3}{4}x - 7 = 5$

Examples

Lesson 2 Write and Solve Two-Step Equations: $p(x + q) = r$

English Learner Instructional Strategy

Collaborative Support: Show What You Know

Organize students into four groups of varying levels of English proficiency. Assign a problem to each group and have them work out the problem together. Then have them describe to each other the steps they performed to write and solve the equation. Finally, for each problem/group, have a student from the group come forward and perform the first step while explaining what they are doing. For example: **I am describing the problem, using only the most important words**. Allow Entering/Emerging students to just do the math or describe the step with a single word or short phrase, such as **multiply**.

English Language Development Leveled Activities

Entering/Emerging	Developing/Expanding	Bridging
Building Oral Language Write $3(x + 7) = -9$ on a large sheet of paper. Organize students into two groups. Give one group an algebra mat and algebra tiles. Give the other group the paper with the equation. Direct the first group to solve the equation for x using manipulatives. Display the following sentence frames: **Add ____. Subtract ____. Multiply by ____. Divide by ____.** As the first group completes each step using the tiles, have them guide the second group in solving the equation on paper. $x = -10$ Write a new equation and have groups switch roles.	**Exploring Language Structure** Assign a problem to student pairs. Have one student guide the other in solving the problem step-by-step. Display the following sentence frames: **Add ____. Subtract ____. Multiply by ____. Divide by ____.** Circulate and listen to students to be sure they are using the present tense. Then have the second student describe the steps they completed using the past tense. **I added ____. I subtracted ____. I multiplied by ____. I divided by ____.** Assign a different problem and have students switch roles.	**Partners Work/Pairs Share** Have partners collaborate to come up with a real-world scenario that would translate into a two-step equation. Monitor and offer feedback as students write out their scenarios. On a separate piece of paper, partners should write the equation and solution to their scenario. Ask partners to trade scenarios with another team who will write and solve the equation. Finally, have pairs come together and discuss each scenario, its equation, and the solution. Does everyone agree?

Teacher Notes:

NAME _____ DATE _____ PERIOD _____

Lesson 2 Notetaking

Write and Solve Two-Step Equations: p(x + q) = r

Use Cornell notes to better understand the lesson's concepts. Complete each sentence by filling in the blanks with the correct word or number.

Questions	Notes
1. How can I use a bar diagram to solve $4(x + 5) = 28$?	Use a <u>bar diagram</u> to help solve the equation: $$\begin{array}{\|c\|c\|c\|c\|} \hline (x+5) & (x+5) & (x+5) & (x+5) \\ \hline \end{array}$$ (with 28 bracketed above) From the diagram, I can tell that one-fourth of 28 is equal to <u>$(x + 5)$</u>. So, I can solve for x: $\dfrac{28}{4} = \dfrac{4(x+5)}{4}$ <u>Division</u> Property of Equality $7 = x + 5$ Simplify. $7 - 5 = x + 5 - 5$ <u>Subtraction</u> Property of Equality $2 = x$ Simplify.
2. How can I use the Properties of Equality to solve $4(x + 5) = 28$?	$4(x + 5) = 28$ $4(x) + 4(5) = 28$ Expand using the <u>Distributive</u> Property. $4x + 20 = 28$ Simplify. $4x + 20 - 20 = 28 - 20$ <u>Subtraction</u> Property of Equality $4x = 8$ Simplify. $\dfrac{4x}{4} = \dfrac{8}{4}$ Division Property of Equality $x = 2$

Summary

Do you prefer using a bar diagram or the Properties of Equality to solve equations? Explain. See students' work.

_____

_____

_____

_____

Module 7 *Equations and Inequalities* **39**

Lesson 3 Write and Solve Equations with Variables on Each Side

English Learner Instructional Strategy

Language Structure Support: Communication Guides

Review the terms *add, subtract, multiply, divide, equation, coefficient, constant,* and *variable.* Ask volunteers to define each, offering an example as support. Prior to beginning a lesson, scan through the lesson to find any vocabulary students might be unfamiliar with and preteach it. When students come upon a word you have taught ahead of time, they may not remember its meaning, but they will likely remember having already heard the word. The more exposure they have ahead of time, the easier it will be when students encounter difficult words, and the more likely students will be to ask for help.

Help students with language that they can use when they need to request help. For example, **Excuse me. May I ask a question? I have a question. I wonder about ____. What is a ____? Is this a ____? I am confused. What is the difference between ____ and ____? I can't remember what ___ means. Can you help me?**

English Language Development Leveled Activities

Entering/Emerging	Developing/Expanding	Bridging
Look, Listen, and Identify	Think-Pair-Share	Exploring Language Structure
Write a story problem on the board and read it with students. For each word in the problem, point to it and ask, *Is this an important word?* When students say **yes,** write down the word. Then use the important words in a sentence that tells what is known. Then use simple words and phrases to guide students to define the variable and write the equation.	Write a story problem on the board or direct students to a problem or example from the module. Ask students to read the problem and identify and list only the most important words. Then have them define the variable and write the equation. Finally, have students turn to another student and compare results. Ask volunteers to share with the group. Tell students that wording might be slightly different, but defining the variable and the equation should be the same.	Review the language for commands. Have students follow your directions as you give commands, such as *Stand up. Raise your hand. Sit down. Smile.* Write an example on the board. Ask, *Is this a complete sentence?* Students might say **no** because there does not appear to be a subject. Tell them that since these are commands, the implied subject is *You.* Have students use this information to write the steps for writing and solving an equation with variables on each side as though they were giving commands to another person. Then have them say the commands to a partner who should follow them.

Teacher Notes:

NAME _____ DATE _____ PERIOD _____

Lesson 3 Review Vocabulary

Write and Solve Equations with Variables on Each Side

Use the vocabulary squares to write a definition, a sentence, and an example for each vocabulary word.

variable	Definition A letter or other symbol used to represent an unspecified number or value
Example Let p = cost of the peaches Let t = the cost of the tomatoes	**Sentence** Sammi defined the variables p and t to represent the costs of peaches and tomatoes.

expression	Definition a group of numbers, variables, and one or more operation that stands for the value of something
Example $5p + 2t$	**Sentence** Sammi wrote an expression to represent the cost of 5 peaches and 2 tomatoes at the farmers' market.

equation	Definition a mathematical sentence stating that two quantities are equal
Example $5p + 2t = c$	**Sentence** Sammi wrote an equation to represent the total cost of buying 5 peaches and 2 tomatoes at the farmers' market.

Lesson 4 Write and Solve Multi-Step Equations

English Learner Instructional Strategy

Collaborative Support: Show What You Know

Organize students into groups of varying levels of English proficiency. Assign a problem to each group and have them work out the problem together. Then have them describe to each other the steps they performed to write and solve the equation. Finally, for each problem/ group, have a student from the group come forward and perform the first step while explaining what they are doing. For example: **I am describing the problem, using only the most important words.** Allow Entering/Emerging students to just do the math or describe the step with a single word or short phrase, such as **multiply.**

English Language Development Leveled Activities

Entering/Emerging	Developing/Expanding	Bridging
Building Oral Language	**Exploring Language Structure**	**Partners Work/Pairs Share**
Write $15(c + 3) + 9 = 2(c + 1)$ on a large sheet of paper. Organize students into two groups. Give one group an algebra mat and algebra tiles. Give the other group the paper with the equation. Direct the first group to solve the equation for c using manipulatives. Display the following sentence frames: **Distribute _____ and _____. Add ____. Subtract ____. Multiply by ____. Divide by ____.** As the first group completes each step using the tiles, have them guide the second group in solving the equation on paper. **($c = -4$)** Write a new equation and have groups switch roles.	Assign a problem to student pairs. Have one student guide the other in solving the problem step-by-step. Display the following sentence frames: **Add ____. Subtract ____. Multiply by ____. Divide by ____. Combine ____. Simplify.** Circulate and listen to students to be sure they are using the present tense. Then have the second student describe the steps they completed using the past tense. **I added ____. I subtracted ____. I multiplied by ____. I divided by ____. I combined ____. I simplified.** Assign a different problem and have students switch roles.	Have partners collaborate to come up with a real-world scenario that would translate into an equation with a variable on each side. Monitor and offer feedback as students write out their scenarios. On a separate piece of paper, partners should write the equation and solution to their scenario. Ask partners to trade scenarios with another team who will write and solve the equation. Finally, have pairs come together and discuss each scenario, its equation, and the solution. Does everyone agree?

Teacher Notes:

NAME _____ DATE _____ PERIOD _____

Lesson 4 Review Vocabulary

Write and Solve Multi-Step Equations

Use the definition map to list qualities about the vocabulary word or phrase.
Sample answers are given.

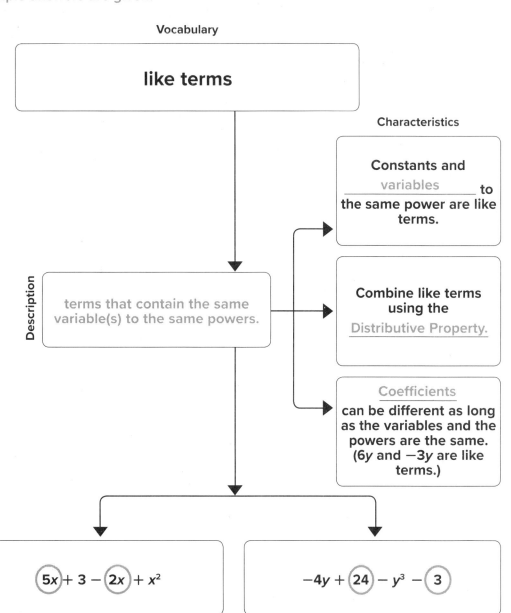

Circle the like terms in each expression.

Lesson 5 Determine the Number of Solutions

English Learner Instructional Strategy

Graphic Support: Graphic Organizer

Help students create a table that they can use for reference when determining the number of solutions to an equation. An equation will have no solution, one solution, or an infinite number of solutions. Show students an example of an equation that has no solution; for example, $5x + 5 = 5(x + 2)$. Take students through the example to see that this equation is impossible to solve because 5 does not equal 10, so there is no value of x that makes this equation work. Repeat for examples that have one solution or infinite solutions. Have students refer to the table as they work through the lesson.

	No Solution	One Solution	Infinite Solution
Symbols	$a \neq b$	$x = a$	$a = a$
Examples	$5x + 5 = 5(x + 2)$ $5 \neq 0$	$5x + 5 = 4(x + 2)$ $x = 3$	$5x + 10 = 5(x + 2)$ $10 = 10$

English Language Development Leveled Activities

Entering/Emerging	Developing/Expanding	Bridging
Developing Oral Language Students may be able to complete the problems without using English. Use their confidence in math as a springboard for helping them produce new English vocabulary. For example, when they determine an equation has no solution, model and prompt the sentence, **It has no solution.** Have students say the sentence chorally and then individually, if possible. For an equation with one solution, use, **It has one solution. x equals ____.** And for an equation with infinite solutions, **It has an infinite number of solutions.**	**Building Oral Language** Repeat the Entering/Emerging activity. Once students have determined the number of solutions mathematically, have them report in English by making a statement, including how they know. For example, model and prompt the sentence, **The equation has no solution because ____. The equation has one solution; x always equals ____. The equation has an infinite number of solutions; it is true for any value of x.**	**Share What You Know** Have Bridging students pair with an Entering/Emerging or Developing/Expanding student and help their peers express themselves in English as they describe the steps for solving an equation. Encourage supportive communication, such as **Your math is correct. Can you describe this step again? You can say ____. This word is pronounced ____. Can you try saying it again?** Remind Bridging mentors that Entering/Emerging students may have very limited ability to respond verbally, but every little bit of practice helps.

Teacher Notes:

NAME _____ DATE _____ PERIOD _____

Lesson 5 Review Vocabulary

Determine the Number of Solutions

Use the three-column chart to organize the vocabulary and key words in this lesson. Write the word in Spanish. Then write the definition of each word.

English	Spanish	Definition
coefficient	coeficiente	The numerical factor of a term that contains a ___variable___
constant	constante	A term without a ___variable___
equation	ecuación	A mathematical sentence stating that two quantities are ___equal___
solution	solución	Any value that satisfies an ___equation___
inverse operations	peraciones inversas	Pairs of operations that ___undo___ each other. For example, multiplication and ___division___ are inverse operations.

42 **Module 7** *Equations and Inequalities*

Lesson 6 Write and Solve One-Step Addition and Subtraction Inequalities

English Learner Instructional Strategy

Graphic Support: Signal Word Chart

Tell students that there are words in problems that signal inequalities. Write the following list of words and phrases on the board: *over, less than, at least, at most, more than, under, below, above, no more than, no less than, up to*. Have students highlight any of these words or phrases they see in the problems.

Have students create a four-column chart in their math notebooks using *greater than* ($>$), *less than* ($<$), *greater than or equal to* ($\geq$), and *less than or equal to* ($\leq$) as column headings. Have partners work together to determine which word or phrase signals which inequality and write it in the appropriate column. Clarify meanings with examples, if necessary.

English Language Development Leveled Activities

Entering/Emerging	Developing/Expanding	Bridging
Look, Listen, and Identify Graph several inequalities on number lines. Copy and distribute to each pair of students. Guide students as they try to determine the inequality represented on the graph by asking simple questions and giving simple directions. For example, say, *Where does the graph begin? Point to that place.* Students point. Ask, *What number is it? Is the graph shaded to the left or right? Is the inequality greater or less than? Is the dot open or closed? So, is the inequality [greater/less] than or equal to?* Remember that students may only be able to point or say **yes** or **no**.	**Look, Say, and Write** Graph several inequalities on number lines. Copy and distribute to each pair of students. Have students write an inequality based on the graph. Encourage students to use the following language as they work: **The dot is open. the number is not equal to _____. It is shaded to the [left/right] of _____. This means we use [greater/less] than. The inequality is _____.** Have students write the inequality mathematically and in words.	**Share What You Know** Partner a Bridging student with an Entering/Emerging or Developing/Expanding student and have them browse the lesson's story problems and identify any troublesome vocabulary. The Bridging student should help the partner determine the meanings of any unknown words by using gestures, pictures, dictionaries, or short phrases as an explanation.

Teacher Notes:

NAME _____ DATE _____ PERIOD _____

Lesson 6 Vocabulary

Write and Solve One-Step Addition and Subtraction Inequalities

Use the vocabulary squares to write a definition, a sentence, and an example for
each vocabulary word.   Sample answers are given.

inequality	Definition
	an open sentence that uses $<$, $>$, $\neq$, $\leq$, or $\geq$ to compare two quantities
Example	**Sentence**
$3x > 5$	The inequality $3x > 5$ is read as three times x is greater than five.

Subtraction Property of Inequality	Definition
	If you subtract the same number from each side of an inequality, the inequality remains true.
Example	**Sentence**
$\begin{aligned} 5 + a &> 15 \\ -5 \quad\;\; &-5 \\ \hline a &> 10 \end{aligned}$	You can use the Subtraction Property of Inequality to solve the inequality $5 + a > 15$. Subtract 5 from each side and simplify to $a > 10$.

Addition Property of Inequality	Definition
	If you add the same number to each side of an inequality, the inequality remains true.
Example	**Sentence**
$\begin{aligned} b - 7 &\leq 10 \\ +7 \quad\; &+7 \\ \hline b &\leq 17 \end{aligned}$	You can use the Addition Property of Inequality to solve the inequality $b - 7 \leq 10$. Add 7 to each side and simplify to $b \leq 17$.

Lesson 7 Write and Solve One-Step Multiplication and Division Inequalities

English Learner Instructional Strategy

Collaborative Support: Act It Out

Write the following real-world problem on the board: *Five players on the soccer team scored goals this season. Eddie scored 3 goals, Max scored 13, Yeshi scored 8, and Aiden scored 9.* Then teach or review this vocabulary from the problem: *goal, soccer team, scored, scorers, season.* Define the words using photos and demonstrations. Have groups of students prepare a skit. Have each student in the group take on one of the following roles: Eddie, Max, Yeshi, or Aiden. Have the "scorers" compare their total number of goals, using the sentence frame, I scored [more/fewer] goals than you scored. Review the difference between *less than* and *fewer than; fewer than* is used with things that can be counted (such as *goals* or *points*). Have each scorer compare to all three of the other scorers and then write an inequality, both mathematically and in words, to describe the relationships.

English Language Development Leveled Activities

Entering/Emerging	Developing/Expanding	Bridging
Developing Oral Language Distribute a number of pennies to each student. Have students count their pennies and then compare numbers with other students. Have them use the sentence frames **I have [more/fewer] pennies than _____. I have as many pennies as _____.**	**Building Oral Language** Repeat the Entering/Emerging activity. After students have mastered the sentence frames with the subject *I,* model and prompt new frames using classmates' names as the subject. For example, **James has [more/fewer] pennies than I do. James has as many pennies as I do.**	**Share What You Know** Have a Bridging student act as a mentor and help an Entering/ Emerging or Developing/Expanding student identify the key words that indicate which inequality symbol to use in each of the problems in the lesson. In the first example in the lesson, for instance, mentors might say, **They key words are *at least $120*. Does that mean greater than $120 or less than $120? Does it include $120 or not?** They should also help the partner make a list of the signal words in their math notebooks.

Teacher Notes:

NAME _____ DATE _____ PERIOD _____

Lesson 7 Vocabulary

Write and Solve One-Step Multiplication and Division Inequalities

Draw a line to connect each inequality to the phrase that best represents it.

$4x < b$

$18q - 23 > r$

less than

$3x - 2y \leq 6z$

less than or equal to

$\frac{1}{2}m \geq 2n$

$6x \leq 13$

greater than

$7a + 14 > 56b$

greater than or equal to

$\frac{4}{7}c \geq \frac{2}{3}d$

Lesson 8 Write and Solve Two-Step Inequalities

English Learner Instructional Strategy

Collaborative Support: Numbered Heads Together

Organize students into groups of four and assign a number 1 to 4 to each student. Have the small groups work together on the following problems: $5x - 7 \geq 43$ and $11 \leq 7 + \frac{x}{5}$. They should discuss each problem, agree on a solution, and ensure that everyone in the group understands and can give the answer. When it is time to review the answer, call out a random number from 1 to 4. The students assigned to that number should raise their hands, and when called on, will answer for the team. Encourage the following language as students work in groups:

Entering/Emerging: **Is this correct? I (don't) understand.**

Developing/Expanding: **Do you get it? I (don't) understand. I can answer this. I (don't) agree.**

Bridging: **Do you think you can answer this? I can give the answer. I'm afraid I don't agree with your answer.**

English Language Development Leveled Activities

Entering/Emerging	Developing/Expanding	Bridging
Developing Oral Language Write the inequalities $3x - 4 \leq 8$, $2x + 5 \geq 15$, $\frac{x}{2} + 5 > 4$, and $\frac{x}{5} - 7 < -3$ on the board. Point to each inequality and say, *This inequality has two* **operations**. Point to the inequality symbol and ask, *What does this mean?* Write these possible responses on the board, and have students point to the correct one: **less than, less than or equal to, greater than, greater than or equal to**. Then ask, *How do I solve the inequality?* Have students respond using these sentence frames: **Subtract ____ from ____. Add ____ to ____. Multiply ____ by ____. Divide ____ by ____.**	**Partners Work/Pairs Share** Divide students into pairs. Then write and read aloud this problem: *A tutoring company charges $60 to enroll plus $20 per session. Moira does not want to spend more than $100 for tutoring. How many tutoring sessions can she have?* Direct partners to write and solve an inequality based on this word problem. **$60 + 20x \leq 100$** Then have them interpret the solution, using this sentence frame: **Moira can have ____ tutoring sessions.** Finally, have them check their answer against that of another pair of students.	**Share What You Know** Direct students to write and solve a two-step inequality of their own. Then have them explain their two-step inequality to an Entering/Emerging or Developing/Expanding peer, guiding their partner through the solution. Permit native language use for clarification. Finally, have the Entering/Emerging or Developing/Expanding student report back to you with the solution.

Teacher Notes:

NAME _____ DATE _____ PERIOD _____

Lesson 8 Vocabulary

Write and Solve Two-Step Inequalities

Use the definition map to list qualities about the vocabulary word or phrase.
Sample answers are given.

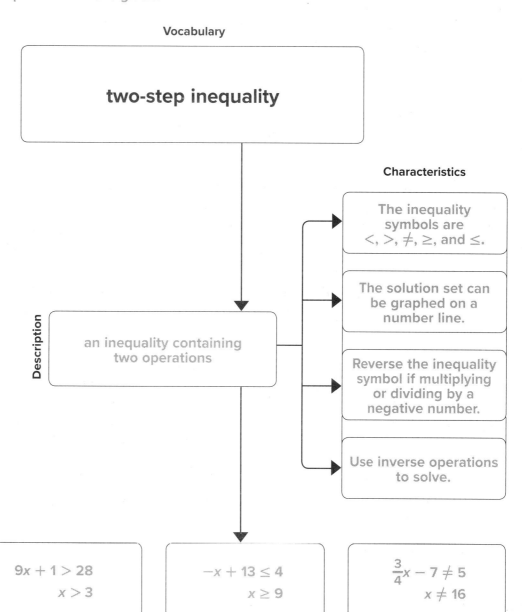

Vocabulary

two-step inequality

Characteristics

The inequality symbols are $<, >, \neq, \geq,$ and $\leq.$

The solution set can be graphed on a number line.

Reverse the inequality symbol if multiplying or dividing by a negative number.

Use inverse operations to solve.

Description

an inequality containing two operations

$9x + 1 > 28$
$x > 3$

$-x + 13 \leq 4$
$x \geq 9$

$\frac{3}{4}x - 7 \neq 5$
$x \neq 16$

Write and solve examples.

Module 7 *Equations and Inequalities* **45**

Lesson 1 Proportional Relationships and Slope
English Learner Instructional Strategy

Graphic Support: Word Webs

Write *linear relationship* and its Spanish cognate, *relación lineal,* on the Word Wall. Provide concrete examples by plotting a linear relationship on a graph.

Use a word web, and write *constant* in the center. Guide students in completing the web with synonyms for *constant* (*same, unchanging, steady*) and examples of constant events (sun rising, seasons, lunar cycles). Repeat for *change* and *rate*.

Display the following sentence frames to help students during the lesson:

The constant rate of change is _____ per _____.

The rate of change is not constant because _____.

English Language Development Leveled Activities

Entering/Emerging	Developing/Expanding	Bridging
Basic Vocabulary	Academic Vocabulary	Act It Out
Create two 2-by-5 tables. Label one table *Weeks* and *Days,* and the other *Months* and *Days.* Refer to a calendar as you read the days of the week and track the total with tally marks. Have students say the days along with you. Use the first table to show a constant rate of change for weeks (1 : 7; 2 : 14; etc.). Then start with the current month and say, _____ *days in* _____. Have students chorally repeat. Continue for five months. Record the data in the second table. Graph both tables to compare a constant rate of change with one that is not constant.	Divide students into two groups. Give one group color tiles and a ruler. Have them measure to the nearest $\frac{1}{4}$-inch as they add three tiles at a time, up to 15 tiles total. Give the other group paper clips and a ruler. Have them measure one paper clip, add two more and measure again, add three more, and so on five times. Have the groups record their data in a table and graph it. Afterward, have groups say whether the change was constant, whether it was a linear relationship, and whether the linear relationship was proportional.	Have pairs of students take turns performing a physical task, such as jumping jacks or sit-ups, for 5 minutes. The partner who is not performing the task will keep time and track the number of actions performed per minute. After each partner has completed the task, ask teams to organize their information in a table and determine the rate of change. Ask them whether the rate of change was constant or not. Have them use the rate to find the number of actions they would have performed in 5 minutes if their rate had remained constant.

Multicultural Teacher Tip

Word problems are an important part of the math curriculum, but they are especially challenging for ELLs. Allow students to share examples from their own cultures, including popular national sports, foods and drinks from their culture, traditional clothing worn in their home countries, and so on. When appropriate, help ELLs reword an exercise to include a familiar cultural reference.

NAME _____ DATE _____ PERIOD _____

Lesson 1 Vocabulary

Proportional Relationships and Slope

Use the word cards to define each vocabulary word or phrase and give an example. Sample answers are given.

Word Cards

linear relationship

Definition

a relationship that has a

straight-line graph

_____

Example Sentence

A store sells sandwiches for $3 each. The relationship between

price and number of sandwiches is a linear relationship.

relación lineal

Definición

relación cuya gráfica es una

recta

_____

- -

Word Cards

constant rate of change

Definition

the rate of change between any two

points in a linear relationship is the

same or constant

Example Sentence

A store sells sandwiches for $3 each. There is a constant rate

of change between the price and number of sandwiches.

tasa constant de cambio

Definición

la tasa de cambio entre dos puntos

cualesquiera en una relación lineal

permanence igual o constante

Lesson 2 Slope of a Line

English Learner Instructional Strategy

Collaborative Support: Echo Reading

Pair Entering/Emerging students with Developing/Expanding or Bridging students. Write *rise, run,* and *slope.* Direct pairs to locate the terms in a glossary or math dictionary and copy the definition for each on a sheet of paper. Have the more proficient English speaker read aloud *rise* and its definition and pass the sheet to the other student. The Entering/Emerging student will read aloud *rise* and, if comfortable, the definition as well. Repeat for other words. Be sure students are differentiating between the /z/ sound in *rise* and the /s/ sound in *slope.*

Distribute paper and a ruler to each pair. Direct them to draw a diagonal line from a vertical side to a horizontal side, creating a right triangle. Say, *Measure the base and height to the nearest inch. Then determine the slope.* Display sentence frames for students to describe the slope:

The rise is _____. The run is _____. The slope is _____.

English Language Development Leveled Activities

Entering/Emerging	Developing/Expanding	Bridging
Frontload Academic Vocabulary Show an image of a sunrise. Point up as you say, *Sunrise. The sun comes up.* Then pretend to be sleeping and then waking. Say, *When I wake up, I rise.* Display a sloping line between two points on a graph. Then draw lines to indicate the rise and run. Draw an upward arrow next to the rise as you say, *Rise.* Have students chorally repeat. In a similar manner, demonstrate *run* by running back and forth before indicating the run on the graph and having students chorally repeat *run.* For *slope,* display an image of a ski slope.	**Report Back** Divide students into pairs. Distribute graph paper to each pair, along with two number cubes. In a hat or other container, place several scraps of paper with either + or − written on them. Say, *Roll your number cubes. Use one number as a rise and the other as a run.* Then have each pair draw a paper from the hat to determine the direction of their slope. Give students time to graph their lines. Then display the following sentence frames for students to report back: **The rise is _____. The run is _____. The slope is _____.**	**Share What You Know** Have students work in pairs. Give each pair a drinking straw and one-inch grid paper with an *x*- and *y*-axis drawn on it. Say, *Drop the straw on the graph paper. Draw a line that follows the straw. Make sure the line goes through two definite points.* Have students label the points, the rise, and the run. Then have students use the points to find the slope of the line. Ask, *If a younger student wanted to know how to find the slope of a line, how would you explain it?* Have volunteers share their answers.

Teacher Notes:

NAME _____ DATE _____ PERIOD _____

Lesson 2 Vocabulary

Slope of a Line

Use the concept web to define slope in five different ways. Sample answers are given.

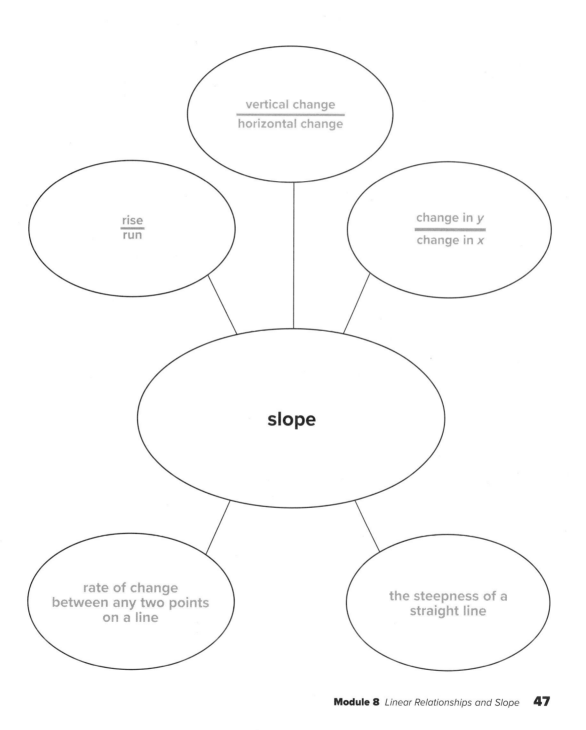

Module 8 *Linear Relationships and Slope* **47**

Lesson 3 Similar Triangles and Slope

English Learner Instructional Strategy

Language Structure Support: Tiered Questions

During the lesson, be sure to ask questions according to ELLs' level of English proficiency. Ask Entering/Emerging students simple questions that elicit one-word answers or allow the student to respond with a gesture: *Is this line the rise or the run? Show me the slope. What are the coordinates of point R? Do I write the ratio as $\frac{1}{2}$ or as $\frac{2}{1}$?* and so on.

For Developing/Expanding students, ask slightly more complex questions: *What do we need to do first? Show me where to draw the line. How would we write the ratio? How do we find the rise?* and so on.

For Bridging students, ask questions that require more complex answers: *How do we determine the slope? Explain how to find the ratio. How do we know these are similar triangles?* and so on.

English Language Development Leveled Activities

Entering/Emerging	Developing/Expanding	Bridging
Word Lists	**Sentence Frames**	**Pairs Work**
Write a comprehensive list of math vocabulary that will be used in this lesson, including *rise, run, vertex, side, slope, ratio, similar, corresponding,* and so on. Have students take turns assisting you in solving problems. During each student's turn, challenge them to use one of the vocabulary words from the list related to the step performed, preferably in a sentence. If a student is reluctant, choose a word for him or her and say it aloud. Have the student echo the word or write it.	Have students work in pairs on the problems you assign. Display the following sentence frames: **The rise is ____. The run is ____. The slope from point ____ to point ____ is ____.** After pairs have finished solving, call on volunteers to use the sentence frames to discuss their answers.	Have students work in pairs to create similar triangles on coordinate grids. Say, *Roll a number cube twice. The first number is the rise, the second number is the run. Draw two slope triangles with that slope.* Allow pairs time to complete the task. Then have them verify the similarity of their triangles mathematically by using the Distance Formula to find the lengths of each side. Have them explain how they know the triangles are similar by determining if the sides are proportional.

Teacher Notes:

NAME _____ DATE _____ PERIOD _____

Lesson 3 Review Vocabulary
Similar Triangles and Slope

Use the word cards to define each vocabulary word or phrase and give an example. Sample answers are given.

Word Cards

slope triangle	triángulo de pediente
Definition	**Definición**
Right triangles that fall on the same line on the coordinate plane.	Triángulos rectos que caen en la misma línea en el plano de coordenadas.

Example Sentence
Slope triangles are similar, so their corresponding sides are proportional.

Word Cards

similar figures	figures semejantes
Definition	**Definición**
Figures that have the same shape but not necessarily the same size.	Figuras que tienen la misma forma pero no necesariamente el mismo tamaño.

Example Sentence
Similar figures have corresponding sides that are proportional and angles that are congruent.

Lesson 4 Direct Variation

English Learner Instructional Strategy

Vocabulary Support: Utilize Resources

Write *direct variation, constant of variation,* and *constant of proportionality* and their Spanish cognates, *variación directa, constante de variación,* and *constante de proporcionalidad,* on the Word Wall and provide concrete examples for each word.

As students work through the lesson, be sure to remind them that they can refer to a glossary or multilingual dictionary for help, or direct students to other translation tools if they are having difficulty with non-math language in the problems, such as *earnings, travel, assume, repair, stain, deck,* and so on.

English Language Development Leveled Activities

Entering/Emerging	Developing/Expanding	Bridging
Non-Transferable Sounds	**Sentence Frames**	**Turn & Talk**
Guide students to create a classroom anchor chart with visual examples for *direct variation, constant of variation,* and *constant of proportionality.* As you provide examples, identify them by saying aloud the corresponding vocabulary phrase, and then have students chorally repeat. Monitor correct pronunciation and repeat the modeling as needed. In particular, listen for the /sh/ sound used in the suffix *-tion.* Native Spanish speakers may default to using the /s/ sound, as /sh/ is not used in Spanish.	Divide students into four groups. Randomly assign a problem to each group. After groups have finished solving, have them use the following sentence frames to share how they arrived at their answers: **First, I needed to know ____. I used the equation y = ____ to represent the ____. I divided ____ to find the value of ____.** Then ask, *What is the slope of your line? What does it tell you about the constant of variation?* After groups determine the slope, have them answer: **The slope is ____, so the constant of variation is also ____.**	Display the following sentence frame: **When a line passes through the origin, I know ____ because ____.** Then display a pair of coordinate planes: one with a line passing through the origin, and one with a line that does not pass through the origin. Ask, *Which of these graphs shows a direct variation? How do you know? Turn to your neighbor and discuss the answer.* Give students a moment to discuss the answer with another student. Then have volunteers use the sentence frame to answer.

Multicultural Teacher Tip

In some cultures, mental math is strongly emphasized. Latin American students in particular may skip intermediate steps when performing algorithms such as long division. Whereas U.S. students are taught to write the numbers they will be subtracting in the process of long division, Latin American students will make the calculations mentally and write only the results.

NAME _____ DATE _____ PERIOD _____

Lesson 4 Vocabulary
Direct Variation

Use the vocabulary squares to write a definition, a sentence, and an example for
each vocabulary word. Sample answers are given.

direct variation	**Definition** the relationship between two variable quantities that have a constant ratio and whose graph passes through the origin
Example The store sells sandwiches for $3 each. The price varies directly with the number of sandwiches.	**Sentence** The relationship between the price of sandwiches and the number of $3 sandwiches is a direct variation.

constant of variation	**Definition** the constant ratio in a direct variation
Example In the direct variation equation $d = 3s$, 3 is the constant of variation.	**Sentence** The store sells sandwiches for $3 each. The constant of variation is 3.

constant of proportionality	**Definition** the constant ratio in a proportional linear relationship
Example In the equation $d = 3s$, 3 is the constant of proportionality.	**Sentence** The store sells sandwiches for $3 each. The constant of proportionality is 3.

Lesson 5 Slope-Intercept Form
English Learner Instructional Strategy

Graphic Support: Charts

Write *intercept* and its Spanish cognate, *interceptar,* on the Word Wall. Discuss math and non-math meanings of *intercept.* If students are familiar with *interception* as a football term, you might relate the sports meaning to the math meaning. Draw two points and connect them with a line. Say, *The quarterback is throwing the ball to the receiver.* Then add an *x*- and *y*-axis so the *y*-axis crosses the line. Say, *But the y-axis comes along and "intercepts" the ball. Where that happens is called the y-intercept.*

Draw a three-column chart labeled *First, Next, Last,* and display the following sentence frames: **The slope is _____. The y-intercept is _____. The equation is _____.** As applicable, have students use the sentence frames to describe how to solve a problem step-by-step. Record each step in the chart.

English Language Development Leveled Activities

Entering/Emerging	Developing/Expanding	Bridging
Look, Listen, and Identify	**Show What You Know**	**Academic Word Knowledge**
Write *slope* and *y-intercept,* say each term aloud as you point to it, and have students chorally repeat. Then have students line up. Write an equation in slope-intercept form below the two terms, point to part of the equation, and ask the first student in line, *Slope or y-intercept?* Have the student answer either verbally or by pointing to the correct term. Have the student write a new equation for the next student in line. After all students have had a turn, show graphs of linear equations and have students identify the *y*-intercepts.	Have students get into groups of four. Write then read aloud, *It costs $7 to get into an international food fair. At each booth, it costs an additional $3 to buy a plate of food. What is the total cost for attending the fair and sampling dishes from 4 booths?* Direct groups to write an equation for the cost of attending the fair and then graph it. $y = 3x + 7$ Display the following sentence frames to help students discuss their answers: **The equation is _____. The slope is _____. The y-intercept is _____. The total cost is _____.**	Divide students into four groups, and distribute three index cards to each group. Write *slope, y-intercept, slope-intercept form.* Say, *Work together in your groups to write a definition for each term on separate index cards.* Afterward, collect the cards. Display the definition found in a dictionary for each term. Randomly choose one of the groups' definitions and lead a discussion comparing it to the dictionary definition.

Teacher Notes:

NAME _____ DATE _____ PERIOD _____

Lesson 5 Vocabulary

Slope-Intercept Form

Use the concept web and the word bank to identify the parts of an equation in slope-intercept form. Sample answers are given.

Word Bank			
slope	*x*-coordinate	*y*-coordinate	*y*-intercept

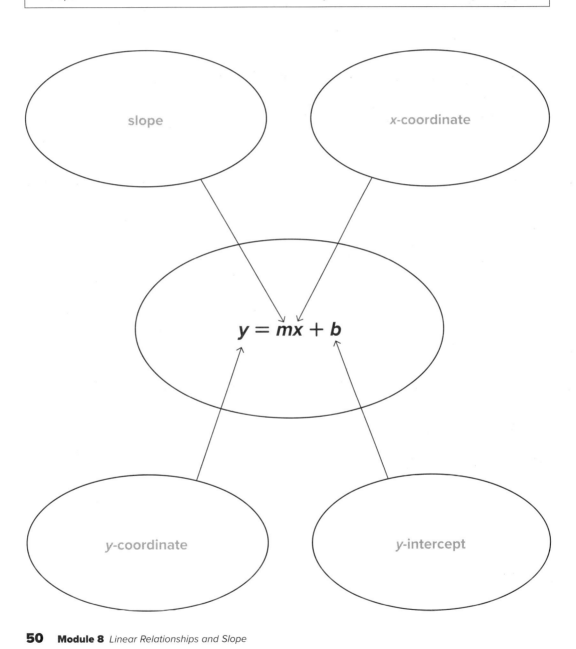

Lesson 6 Graph Linear Equations
English Learner Instructional Strategy

Language Structure Support: Tiered Questions

Before students begin the lesson and watch the lesson video for graphing, preteach or review the following terms: *graph, x-axis, y-axis, point, ordered pair, rise, run, slope, y-intercept, slope-intercept form, unit*. Display a graph and use it to review the terms. Check students' understanding by asking questions that are appropriate to each group.
For example:

Entering/Emerging: Point to the *x*-axis. Ask, *Is this the x-axis?* **yes**

Developing/Expanding: Point to the *x*-axis. Ask, *What is this?* **x-axis**

Bridging: Say, *Show us the x-axis and describe it*. (Students point to the *x*-axis and say, **The x-axis is the horizontal number line on a coordinate plane.**)

English Language Development Leveled Activities

Entering/Emerging	Developing/Expanding	Bridging
Look, Listen, and Identify	**Listen and Identify**	**Academic Word Knowledge**
Draw a picture of the sun low in the sky and then getting higher and higher. Say, *The sun rises*. Say *rise* again and have students repeat. Point to the pictures of the sun going up and ask, *Does it rise?* **yes** Next, draw a standing stick figure and another one that is running. Say, *He runs*. Say *run* again and have students repeat it. Point to the running figure and ask, *Does he run?* **yes** Display a coordinate plane. Start at a point and move two units up. Ask, *Rise or run?* **rise** Move two units right and ask, *Rise or run?* **run** Repeat until students are firm in understanding the concepts. If they become confused, return to the images of the rising sun and the running man to remind students of the correct direction.	Play a vocabulary game. Have partners work as a team. Give a clue about each term used in the Instructional Strategy above. Call on a pair of students. If they can name the term after the first clue, award five points. If they name it after the second clue, award three points. If they need three clues to name the correct term, they receive one point. Use clues such as, *It names a point*. **ordered pair** *It is a vertical number line*. **y-axis**	Review the language for commands. Have students follow your directions as you give commands, such as *Stand up. Raise your hand. Sit down. Smile*. Write an example on the board. Ask, *Is this a complete sentence?* Students might say **no** because there does not appear to be a subject. Tell them that since these are commands, the implied subject is *You*. Have students use this information to write the steps for graphing an equation in slope-intercept form as though they were giving commands to another person. Then have them say the commands to a partner who should follow them. Alternatively, they could give directions to a Developing/Expanding partner.

Teacher Notes:

NAME _____ DATE _____ PERIOD _____

Lesson 6 Notetaking

Graph Linear Equations

Use Cornell notes to better understand the lesson's concepts. Complete each sentence by filling in the blanks with the correct word or phrase.

Questions	Notes
1. What is the equation of a horizontal line? What does the graph of the line look like?	The equation of a horizontal line is y = b, where *b* is the value of the y-coordinates. A horizontal line is **(curved, straight)** and parallel to the x -axis.
2. What is the equation of a vertical line? What does the graph of the line look like?	The equation of a vertical line is x = a, where *a* is the value of the x-coordinates. A vertical line goes straight up and $down$ and is parallel to the y -axis.

Summary

How does the equation of a line written in slope-intercept form help you graph the line?

See students' work.

Lesson 1 Find Likelihoods

English Learner Instructional Strategy

Vocabulary Support: Communication Guides

Write the following on the board: *certain, impossible, likely, unlikely,* and *equally likely.*
Introduce or review each word, and ask students to provide examples of each, if possible.
Prompt them with questions such as *What event is certain?* Assist with ideas as necessary.

Write a variety of events on the board, such as: *The sun will (not) rise tomorrow. I will play
basketball this afternoon. You can roll a 27 on a number cube. A dog will chase a cat. A cat
will chase a dog. One plus one equals three. A coin will land on heads or tails.*

Have students use this sentence frame to report about each scenario: **It is [certain/
impossible/likely/equally likely/unlikely] that ____.**

English Language Development Leveled Activities

Entering/Emerging	Developing/Expanding	Bridging
Basic Vocabulary Write *unlikely* on the board. Review the meaning of *likely* ("a good chance something will happen"). Then underline *un-*. Ask, *What does this word part mean?* **not** Have students give other examples. If they need help, offer *unhappy* or *unknown*. **Note:** The prefix *un-* can also mean "to do the opposite of," as in *untie* or *undo*.	**Listen and Identify** Say a scenario, such as, *When I flip a coin, it will be heads or tails.* Students should use one of the following words to describe the probability: *certain, impossible, likely, unlikely,* and *equally likely.* The first student who correctly answers **certain** gets to come up with the next scenario. Monitor and offer feedback as necessary.	**Build Oral Language** Repeat the Developing/Expanding activity with the following adjustment: instead of making a statement about a scenario, have students formulate a question. Some questions could be fairly complicated, so offer constructive feedback as necessary. Examples include, **What is the likelihood that ____? Is it [certain/ impossible/likely...] that ____? Do you think that ____?**

Teacher Notes:

NAME _____ DATE _____ PERIOD _____

Lesson 1 Vocabulary
Find Likelihoods

Use the vocabulary squares to write a definition, a sentence, and an example for each vocabulary word. Sample answers are given.

	Definition
likelihood	the possibility that something will happen
Example	**Sentence**
The likelihood of rolling a 1 on a number cube is unlikely	The likelihood that the sun will rise tomorrow is certain.

	Definition
outcome	any one of the possible results of an action
Example	**Sentence**
4 is an outcome when a number cube is rolled.	When a number cube is rolled, there are 6 possible outcomes.

	Definition
event	the desired outcome or set of outcomes
Example	**Sentence**
Rolling a 7 on a single number cube is an impossible event.	In the event that Kevin rolls a 2, he will lose the game.

Lesson 2 Relative Frequency of Simple Events
English Learner Instructional Strategy

Vocabulary Support: Multiple-Meaning Words

Before the lesson, write *relative frequency* and its Spanish cognate, *frecuencia relativa*. Introduce the words, and provide math examples. Utilize other translation tools for non-Spanish speaking ELLs. Post the words on the Word Wall. Next, discuss multiple meanings for both *relative* and *frequency*. Help students remember how these words are used in a statistics context by showing and explaining that the *frequency* of an event is how *often* the event happens. Then write: *relate, relative*. Tell students that *relate* is the base word of *relative*. Show and explain how two things that are *relative* to each other *relate,* or *connect,* to each other somehow. Finally, guide students to see how *relative frequency* shows a relationship between how often an event happens in a certain number of attempts.

English Language Development Leveled Activities

Entering/Emerging	Developing/Expanding	Bridging
Number Sense	**Act It Out**	**Share What You Know**
Roll a number cube. Show and write the number. Ask, *What are the possible numbers I can roll?* **1, 2, 3, 4, 5, 6** Next, discuss the probability of rolling each number, given 6 chances to roll. Guide students to tell you the probability is $\frac{1}{6}$. Then ask, *What is the probability of rolling a 3 **or** a 6?* Guide students to tell you the probability of rolling one of these two numbers is $\frac{2}{6}$. Now, write and say: *You will roll the number cube 600 times. The **probability** of rolling a 3 or a 6 is $\frac{2}{6}$. How many rolls will be a 3 or a 6?* Have students respond by solving this proportion: $\frac{2\ rolls}{6\ rolls} = \frac{x\ rolls}{600\ rolls}$. **200 rolls** Repeat to find the probability of rolling a 2, 4 or 6.	Repeat the Entering/Emerging activity. Then have each student roll a number cube six times and record each number. Share results as a class. Report results using this sentence frame: **[Student Name] rolls a 3 or 6 ____ times out of 6 rolls.** Then record the class's results using this sentence frame: **The class rolls ____ times out of [number of students times 6] rolls.** Discuss whether the class results show that the relative frequency of rolling a 3 or 6 gets closer to $\frac{2}{6}$ as the number of rolls increases. Repeat the activity to find out what happens as more rolls are added.	Have partners write a relative frequency scenario. After you check the scenario to ensure it makes sense, tell students to use the scenario to create a presentation for how to find relative frequency. Have them write out a script for their presentation, using the animation in the lesson as a guide, if necessary. Then have them present their lessons to the group.

Teacher Notes:

NAME _____ DATE _____ PERIOD _____

Lesson 2 Vocabulary
Relative Frequency of Simple Events

Use the definition map to list qualities about the vocabulary word or phrase.
Sample answers are given.

Vocabulary

> ### relative frequency

Characteristics:

When you conduct a probability experiment, such as tossing a coin, an ___event___ occurs.

Description

A ratio that compares the frequency of each category to the total

___Probability___ is the chance that an event will occur.

___Relative frequency___ is the number of favorable outcomes to the total number of outcomes in a ___probability experiment___.

A number cube with sides labeled 1, 2, 3, 4, 5, and 6 is rolled 50 times. A 6 is rolled 15 times. What is the relative frequency of rolling a 6? **30%**

A spinner is spun 25 times. It lands on red 3 times. What is the relative frequency of the spinner landing on red? **12%**

Write each relative frequency as a percent.

Lesson 3 Theoretical Probability of Simple Events

English Learner Instructional Strategies

Vocabulary Support: Build Background Knowledge

Write the following terms and their Spanish cognates: *uniform probability model (modelo de probabilidad uniforme), theoretical probability (probabilidad teórica), complementary events (eventos complemetarios),* and *sample space (espacio muestral).* Introduce the words, and provide math examples. Utilize other translation tools for non-Spanish speaking ELLs.

Then write: *theory/theoretical.* Show and explain that the first word is a base word and the second word is formed by adding the suffix *-al.* Discuss how a theory explains events in the natural world and an experiment tests the theory. Finally, tell students that *-al* means "relating to." Guide students to create definitions for *theoretical,* using their base word and suffix meanings. **relating to a theory** Repeat for *probable/probability* where the suffix *-ity* means "state of" or "degree of."

English Language Development Leveled Activities

Entering/Emerging	Developing/Expanding	Bridging
Word Knowledge	Report Back	Public Speaking Norms
Write: *uniform.* Underline *uni.* Show and explain that *uni-* is a prefix meaning "one" and that, when it is added to *form,* it creates a word meaning "one form." Discuss both the noun and adjective definitions of *uniform.* Show photos of people in matching uniforms. Point to each person in the group and say, *This person wears a* **uniform.** Then say, *All the clothes have* **one** *form. Do all the clothes look the* **same** *or* **different**? **same** Then write: *uniform probability model.* Say, *The* **probability model** *shows outcomes. The outcomes are* **uniform**. *Does each outcome have the* **same** *probability of happening?* **yes**	Ask partners to look through a newspaper or on the Internet for college or high school sports statistics. For example, a free-throw average in basketball might be reported as a player having made 6 out of 10 shots. Or, a baseball batting average might be reported with a number such as .245, or 24.5%—this means that for every 1,000 at bats, the player should get a hit 245 times. For each example of sports statistics found, have partners discuss whether it shows theoretical or not. Then have them report their ideas to the class.	Ask, *What is the difference between* **relative frequency** *and* **theoretical probability**? *How are they similar? Can one be used to determine the other?* Have partners discuss their ideas. Then ask partners to share their ideas with the class.

Teacher Notes:

NAME _____ DATE _____ PERIOD _____

Lesson 3 Vocabulary

Theoretical Probability of Simple Events

Use the three-column chart to organize the vocabulary in this lesson.
Write the word in Spanish. Then write the correct terms to complete each
definition.

English	Spanish	Definition
complementary events	eventos complementarios	The events of one outcome happening and that outcome not happening. The ____sum____ of the probabilities of an ____event____ and its complement is 1 or 100%.
sample space	espacio muestral	The set of all possible outcomes of a _probability experiment_
theoretical probability	probabilidad teórica	The ratio of the number of ways an ____event____ can occur to the number of possible outcomes. It is based on what ___should___ happen when conducting a probability experiment.
uniform probability model	modelo de probabilidad uniforme	A probability model which assigns ____equal____ probability to all outcomes

Lesson 4 Compare Probabilities of Simple Events

English Learner Instructional Strategies

Graphic Support: Tables and Graphs

Tables and graphs are excellent for helping students visualize probability. Using either a spinner or a number cube, have partners conduct a probability experiment by performing 20 trials. Have them make a tally chart (table) and calculate the number of outcomes for each possible event. Then have them use the tally chart to create a graph of the results. Tell students the result for each event is the **relative probability.** Ask a student how they can use this information predict the result if they would perform 200 trials.

English Language Development Leveled Activities

For the activities below, draw a bar graph similar to the one shown:

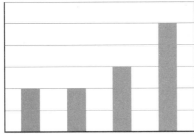

Example 1 Example 2 Example 3 Example 4

Entering/Emerging	Developing/Expanding	Bridging
Look and Identify	**Sentence Frames**	**Building Oral Language**
Review the terms *greater/less than, higher/lower than, equally likely,* and *same.* Refer to the bar graph above. Say, *Compare these examples. Which has the greatest probability? Which two examples are the same?* After doing a few examples, point to two columns and say, *Compare these examples.* Students should use available language and gesturing (such as pointing) to communicate their comparison.	Repeat the Entering/Emerging activity. Offer sentence frames for student to use for comparing the columns: **____ and ____ are equally likely. The probability of ____ is [greater/higher/less/lower] than the probability of ____.**	Have each student select one of the problems from the lesson and use available language to describe how to find the relative frequency for each outcome. Then have them compare the relative frequencies among the different possible outcomes. Make sure they use the terms *greater than, higher than, less than, lower than, equal.*

Teacher Notes:

NAME _____ DATE _____ PERIOD _____

Lesson 4 Notetaking

Compare Probabilities of Simple Events

Use Cornell notes to better understand the lesson's concepts. Complete each sentence by filling in the blanks with the correct word or phrase.

Questions	Notes
1. What is the difference between theoretical probability and relative frequency?	_____Theoretical probability_____ is based on what **should** happen when conducting a probability experiment. _____Relative frequency_____ is what **actually** happens when any probability experiment is conducted.
2. What happens to the relative frequency in a probability experiment when the number of trials increases?	In a probability experiment, as the number of trial increases, the relative frequency becomes closer to the _____theoretical probability_____.

Summary
How did what you already know about relative frequency and theoretical probability help you with this lesson? See students' work. _____ _____ _____ _____ _____ _____ _____ _____

Lesson 5 Probability of Compound Events

English Learner Instructional Strategy

Graphic Support: Graphic Organizers

Before the lesson, write *compound event* and its Spanish cognate, *evento compuesto*. Introduce the words, and provide math examples. Utilize other translation tools for non-Spanish speaking ELLs. Post the words on a Word Wall.

Then write: *tree diagram.* Have students tell about different diagrams they have used in the past. Show examples, such as a Venn diagram or a plant diagram from a science textbook. Discuss how diagrams summarize and organize information. Then show a photo of a tree, along with examples of tree diagrams. Have students tell how the tree diagrams are similar to a tree. **Both have branches.** Then show how the "branches" in a tree diagram "stem" from one term, which names a characteristic the branches share.

English Language Development Leveled Activities

Use the following problem with the leveled activities: *Ming rolls a number cube, tosses a coin, and chooses a card from two cards marked A and B. If an even number and heads appears, Ming wins, no matter which card is chosen. Otherwise, Lashonda wins. Find P (Ming wins).* **25%**

Entering/Emerging	Developing/Expanding	Bridging
Collaborative Support	**Turn and Talk**	**Partners Work/Pairs Check**
Have students work with a multilingual mentor on problems assigned during the lesson. Ask the mentor to help break each problem into parts. For example, for the problem above, have the mentor help the Entering/Emerging student identify these conditions for each turn in Ming's game: *1) A number cube is rolled. There are 6 possible results (rolling 1, 2, 3, 4, 5, or 6). 2) A coin is tossed. There are 2 possible results (heads or tails). 3) A card is drawn. There are 2 possible results (A or B).* Then have the student and mentor work together to set up the sample space.	Have students turn and talk with a neighbor about how to solve the problem. Encourage students to make notes about the ideas they share. Then have them respond to the question individually, using this sentence frame: **The probability that Ming will win is _____ because _____.**	Have pairs review the problem. Then ask partners to work together to write their own word problem. Tell them the word problem must be based on a game and its solution must involve setting up a sample space to find the probability of Player 1 or Player 2 winning. After students have written their problems, have them exchange papers with another pair. Tell partners to work together to solve the problem they receive. Then have them check answers with the pair who wrote the original problem.

Teacher Notes:

NAME _____ DATE _____ PERIOD _____

Lesson 5 Vocabulary
Probability of Compound Events

Use the flow chart to review the process for creating a tree diagram for a compound event. Sample answers are given.

Define the phrase **compound event**.

an event consisting of

two or more simple events

Compound Event

A sandwich can be made with whole wheat or whole grain bread and three kinds of filling: peanut butter, cheese, or tuna salad.

Define the phrase **sample space**.

the set of all possible outcomes

of a probability experiment

List the Sample Space for the Compound Event

Use W for whole wheat, G for whole grain, P for peanut butter, C for cheese, and T for tuna salad.

WP, WC, WT, GP, GC, GT

Define the phrase **tree diagram**.

a diagram used to show the

sample space

Complete the tree diagram.

Bread	Filling	Sample Space
	P	WP
W	C	WC
	T	WT
	P	GP
G	C	GC
	T	GT

Lesson 6 Simulate Chance Events

English Learner Instructional Strategy

Sensory Support: Videos, Films, and Broadcasts

Before the lesson, write *simulation* and its Spanish cognate, *simulación*. Introduce the words, and provide math examples. Utilize other translation tools for non-Spanish speaking ELLs. Write: *simulate, simulation*. Explain that: 1) *Simulate,* a verb, is the base word of *simulation,* a noun. Use each word in a context sentence. 2) *Simulate* and *simulation* share the root word *sim,* which means "like." Discuss how the meaning "like" relates to the meanings of these words, as well as others with *sim,* such as *similar* and *simile*. Finally, show students videos of simulations and discuss how they are like dress rehearsals or re-enactments—they imitate real-life to help us prepare for the future (NASA's flight simulations for astronauts) or understand how something happened in the past (computer simulations).

English Language Development Leveled Activities

Entering/Emerging	Developing/Expanding	Bridging
Cooperative Learning	**Communication Guides**	**Show What You Know**
Have students work with a multilingual mentor on problems during the lesson. Ask the mentor to help students identify the conditions for each simulation and reword them, using simpler language. Then have students describe a model for simulating the outcome requested in the problem, using their native language. Have the mentors help students translate their ideas.	For each sample problem, show and discuss how each situation includes a set of conditions and a probability question. Ask partners to work together to brainstorm situations that could be represented by a simulation. Have partners choose a situation to describe and an outcome to simulate, using this communication guide: **These are the conditions: 1) ____; 2) ____; 3) ____. We want to know the probability of ____. We will use ____ to simulate the outcome. We will simulate the outcome by ____.**	Have partners choose a problem to work on together. Ask them to 1) identify the word problem's conditions and probability question, 2) discuss possible models for simulating the requested outcome, and 3) choose a model to describe. Have them make notes about how they chose their model. Then have them present their problem and solution to the class.

Multicultural Teacher Tip

Word problems are an important part of the math curriculum, but they can be particularly challenging for ELLs. Allow students to share examples from their own cultures, including popular national sports, foods and drinks from their culture, traditional clothing worn in their home countries, and so on. When appropriate, help ELLs reword an exercise to include a familiar cultural reference.

NAME _____ DATE _____ PERIOD _____

Lesson 6 Vocabulary

Simulate Chance Events

Use the concept web to define simulation. Then give examples of different
simulations from the book. Sample answers are given.

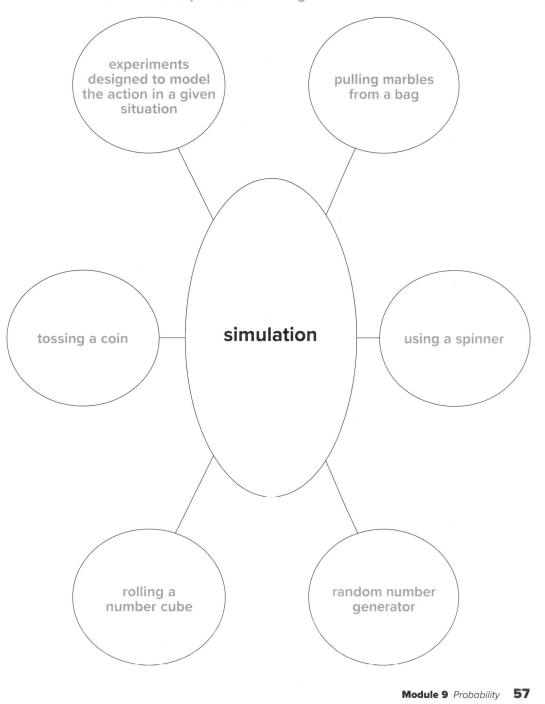

Lesson 1 Biased and Unbiased Samples

English Learner Instructional Strategy

Vocabulary Support: Activate Prior Knowledge

Before the lesson, write: *bias, biased, unbiased*. Ask, *How can a game show* ***bias?*** **One player has a better chance of winning than another player.** Next, underline the common letters in *biased* and *unbiased* to show that *bias* is their base word. Circle the *-ed* ending on *biased* and *unbiased*, and tell students this ending can be used to make some nouns into adjectives. Discuss how *biased* describes results that are *not fair*. Use the word in a context sentence that demonstrates its meaning. Finally, circle the *un* in *unbiased* and tell students these letters form the prefix *un-*, meaning "not." Ask, *What kind of results does* ***unbiased*** *describe?* **results that are fair** Use *unbiased* in a context sentence that demonstrates its meaning.

English Language Development Leveled Activities

Entering/Emerging	Developing/Expanding	Bridging
Act It Out	**Synthesis**	**Word Knowledge**
Write: *random*. Say the word with students. As needed, demonstrate how to say /r/ (a sound not used in some languages) by isolating the sound and having students repeat. Next, write the following lists: 1) 1, 3, 2, 4; 2) 1, w, 6, x, z, 5; 3) a, a, b, b, c, c; 4) *, &, #, %, *, ^. Point to the group of items in list 1. Ask, *Is there a* ***pattern?*** **yes** Help students describe the pattern. Then say, *There* ***is*** *a pattern. This is* ***not*** *random.* Then point to list 2. Ask, *Is there a* ***pattern?*** **no** Discuss why. Then say, *There* ***is not*** *a pattern. This is* ***random.*** Continue in the same way with lists 3 and 4, which are **not random** and **random,** respectively.	Write these questions on the board: 1) *What is* ***simple*** *about a* ***Simple*** *Random Sample?* 2) *What is the* ***system*** *for taking a* ***Systematic*** *Random Sample?* 3) *What do a* ***Convenience*** *Sample and a* ***convenience*** *store have in common?* 4) *How do* ***volunteers*** *help with a* ***Voluntary*** *Response Sample?* Have students write their responses. Allow them to turn and talk to a neighbor, as needed, for help with fleshing out an idea or phrasing an answer. Then ask them to discuss their answers to the questions as a class.	Have students help you write a definition for *bias* that uses their own words. Then write: *tendency, prejudice*. Ask partners to find the meanings for *tendency* and *prejudice* and discuss what they have to do with *bias*. Then have them write a sentence of two that explains how the words are related. Finally, ask students to share their sentences with the class.

Teacher Notes:

NAME _____ DATE _____ PERIOD _____

Lesson 1 Vocabulary

Biased and Unbiased Samples

Use the three-column chart to organize the vocabulary in this lesson. Write the word in Spanish. Then write the definition of each word. Sample answers are given.

English	Spanish	Definition
unbiased sample	muestra no sesgada	a sample representative of the entire population
simple random sample	muestra aleatoria simple	an unbiased sample where each item or person in the population is as likely to be chosen as any other
systematic random sample	muestra aleatoria sistemática	a sample where the items or people are selected according to a specific time or item interval
biased sample	muestra sesgada	a sample drawn in such a way that one or more parts of the population are favored over others
convenience sample	muestra de conveniencia	a sample which consists of members of a population that are easily accessed
voluntary response sample	muestra de repuesta voluntaria	a sample which involves only those who want to participate in the sampling

Lesson 2 Make Predictions

English Learner Instructional Strategy

Vocabulary Support: Cognates

Before the lesson, write *population* and *statistics* and their Spanish cognates, *población* and *estadistica,* respectively. Introduce the words, and provide math examples. Utilize other translation tools for non-Spanish speaking ELLs. Post the words on a Word Wall. Underline *pop* in *population.* Tell students that *pop* is a root word that means "people." Help students relate the meaning of the root word to the meaning of *population.* Share examples of other words with *pop,* such as *popular* and *populous,* and relate their meanings to the meaning of the root. Finally, have students write their own definitions for *population* and *statistics* in their notebooks. Encourage them to include with each definition a sentence, using the vocabulary word in context, and an illustration to help them remember the word's meaning.

English Language Development Leveled Activities

Entering/Emerging	Developing/Expanding	Bridging
Basic Vocabulary	**Act It Out**	**Public Speaking Norms**
Before the lesson, show and explain the meanings of these words, found in this lesson's word problems: *athletic, baseball, softball, basketball, football, gymnastics, tennis, volleyball, defects, Smart watches, non-profit, volunteer, lasagna, jeans, capris, athletic pants, banana, blueberry, honeydew.* Teaching students this basic vocabulary prior to the lesson will help them to focus their attention on instruction during the lesson.	Have partners work together to brainstorm survey questions they could use to find out more about their classmates' interests or preferences. After they have had some time to think, tell partners to choose one question to write and then pass their question around for classmates to answer. Once their surveys have circulated throughout the class, have partners chart the responses in a table they create. Finally, have them find the probability for each survey response, based on their sample.	Ask, *What is a prediction?* **Sample response: A statement telling something that is likely to happen in the future.** Then post these questions: *What are examples of predictions you have heard people make? On what facts did the people base their predictions? When and why might you make a prediction? What makes predictions reliable? How can mathematics make a prediction more reliable?* Have students discuss their responses to these questions with a neighbor. Then ask them to share their ideas and experiences with the class.

Teacher Notes:

NAME _____ DATE _____ PERIOD _____

Lesson 2 Vocabulary
Make Predictions

Use the vocabulary squares to write a definition, a sentence, and an example for each vocabulary word. Sample answers are given.

statistics	**Definition** the study of collecting, organizing, and interpreting data
Example Sixty-five percent of the students surveyed said their favorite subject is math.	**Sentence** Using statistics, you can get information about a population and find trends in data.

survey	**Definition** a question or set of questions designed to collect data about a specific group of people, or population
Example 1. What grade are you in? 2. Who is your teacher? 3. Do you prefer pizza or pasta?	**Sentence** The survey included questions about grade, teacher, and food.

population	**Definition** the entire group of items or individuals from which the samples under consideration are taken
Example 7th graders at Beacon Middle School	**Sentence** The population included all 7th grade students in the school.

Lesson 3 Generate Multiple Samples

English Learner Instructional Strategy

Graphic Support: Graphic Organizers

Draw a *Mean* definition web on an anchor chart or word wall. Help students complete the web by writing a definition for the statiscal mean, listing characteristics of the mean, and showing examples of how to find the mean. Tell students that in this lesson, they will be finding the mean of more than one set of numbers, or the mean of multiple samples of the same population.

For *variability,* have volunteers draw an example graph for one of the following: *high variability, low variability, no variability.* Ask students to use available language to describe each graph.

Entering/Emerging students can point, say yes/no, or give short responses.

Developing/Expanding students can use simple sentences: **The first graph shows _____.**

Bridging students can use more complex language: **The first graph shows _____ because _____.**

English Language Development Leveled Activities

Entering/Emerging	Developing/Expanding	Bridging
Look, Listen, and Identify	**Listen and Identify**	**Academic Vocabulary**
Draw examples of *high, low,* and *no variability.* Ask, *Which one shows high variability?* Students should point to the correct graph. When they have identified the correct graph, model and prompt students to say **high variability.** Repeat until students are firm in their understanding and can clearly pronounce each term.	Give clues about any of the following vocabulary and have students identify the term: *biased sample, unbiased sample, convenience sample, voluntary response sample, variability, high/low/no variability.* For example, say, *All responses in the sample are the same.* **no variability** Depending on students' abilities, challenge them to provide the clues to a partner.	Have students create or add to an anchor chart to cover all of the words learned in the module so far. Assign one or more words to each student and have them write the word, its cognate, a definition, and an example for each term. Then have them share their work with a partner to discuss any revisions. Finally share with the group before adding the information to the anchor chart.

Teacher Notes:

NAME _____ DATE _____ PERIOD _____

Lesson 3 Vocabulary
Generate Multiple Samples

Use the definition map to list qualities about the vocabulary word or phrase.
Sample answers are given.

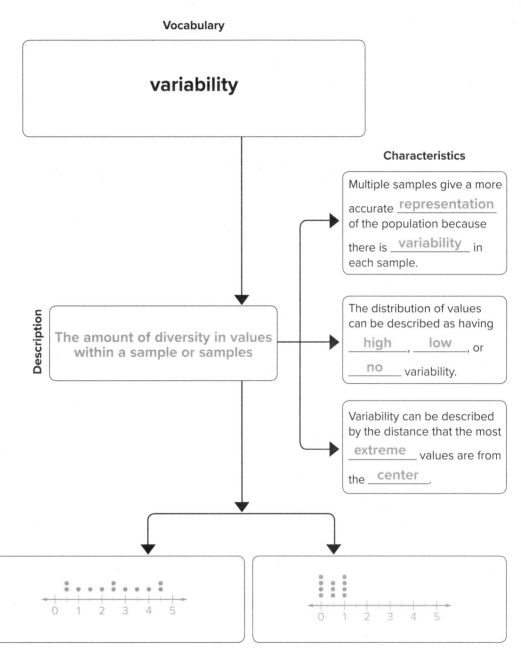

Vocabulary

variability

Characteristics

Multiple samples give a more accurate representation of the population because there is variability in each sample.

The distribution of values can be described as having high, low, or no variability.

Variability can be described by the distance that the most extreme values are from the center.

Description

The amount of diversity in values within a sample or samples

Examples of two dot plots with different variability.

Lesson 4 Compare Two Populations

English Learner Instructional Strategy

Graphic Support: Graphs

Before the lesson, write: *first quartile, third quartile, interquartile range.* Discuss how these terms are related. First, underline the letters *quart* in each of the terms, and tell students these letters form a root word meaning "one-fourth." Next, write: 1, 2, 3, 3, 3, 4, 5. Ask, *What is the **median**?* **3** Then use the number list to show that a *quartile* is the median of the numbers before or after the median number—the *first quartile* is the median of 1 and 3, and the *third quartile* is the median of 3 and 5. Discuss how the *median,* or *middle* number, cuts the number list in *one-half,* and the quartile numbers cut each *half* into *one-fourth.* Finally, draw a box-plot graph that shows the median, first quartile, and third quartile for your number list. Show how the *Interquartile Range* is the range *between* the first and third quartilies.

English Language Development Leveled Activities

Entering/Emerging	Developing/Expanding	Bridging/Reteaching
Word Knowledge	Make Connections	Anchor Chart
Write: *symmetric.* Underline the letters *sym* and explain that these letters form a root word that means "same." Draw a simple symmetric and non-symmetric box plot on the board. Point to the symmetric box plot example. Ask, *What is the **same**?* Guide students to show or tell you that the distance between the first quartile and median points is the same as the distance between the median and third quartile points. Then discuss why the box plot in the second example is not symmetric. Show and say, *These distances are **not** symmetric. They are **not** the **same**.*	Write these words: *quartile, quarter, quartet.* Ask, *What root word do these words have in common?* **quart** *What does the root word mean?* **one-fourth** Then have students work with a neighbor. Tell them to find the meaning of each word on the board and then write a sentence telling how the meaning of the word and its root are related. Have them use this sentence frame: **The meaning of [*quartile/quarter/ quartet*] is like the meaning of *quart* because _____.**	Have students work as a group to create a graffiti poster that helps further explain the concept of Mean Absolute Deviation. Explain that the poster should include the following: 1) math definitions for these terms: *mean, absolute value, deviation, difference, average;* 2) numbered steps for finding the mean absolute deviation of a data set; and 3) an example problem. Encourage students to make their poster fun and colorful. Discuss their finished poster with the class.

Teacher Notes:

NAME _____ DATE _____ PERIOD _____

Lesson 4 Vocabulary
Compare Two Populations

Use the word cards to define each vocabulary word or phrase and give an example. Sample answers are given.

Word Cards

| **double box plot** | **doble diagram de caja** |

Definition

two box plots graphed on the

same number line

_____

Example Sentence

You can draw inferences about two populations using a double

box plot to compare their centers and variations.

Definición

dos diagramas de caja sobre

la misma recta numérica

_____

Word Cards

| **double dot plot** | **doble diagram de puntos** |

Definition

a distribution of two sets of data

values where each value is shown

as a dot above a number line

Example Sentence

A double dot plot uses the same number line to draw

inferences about two populations.

Definición

una distribución de dos conjuntos

de valores donde cada valor se

muestra como un punto arriba de

una recta numérica

Lesson 5 Assess Visual Overlap

English Learner Instructional Strategy

Vocabulary Support: Build Background Knowledge

Write *visual overlap* on the board or Word Wall. Ask, *What does* visual *mean?* Give students a chance to answer. Then, if necessary, say, *Visual describes something related to sight or that can be seen.* Then demonstrate the meaning of *overlap* using two sheets of paper. Slide one sheet partly over the other and point to where they overlap. Say, *This part of the paper* **overlaps** *the other part.* **Overlap** *is the area where one thing partly covers another thing.* Say, *Visual overlap means you can see where the overlap is.* Say *visual overlap* and have students chorally repeat.

Write *assess* on the board and provide more familiar synonyms or related phrases to help clarify the meaning, such *evaluate, estimate, get an idea of, judge, consider.* Provide a nonmath example of *assess,* such as assessing a situation: *I can* **assess** *the weather by looking outside to see what the sky looks like, what other people are wearing, how strong the wind is blowing.* Explain that to *assess visual overlap* means comparing two sets of data to get an idea of how similar or different the means are likely to be.

English Language Development Leveled Activities

Entering/Emerging	Developing/Expanding	Bridging
Word Knowledge	Echo Reading	Round the Table
Review *mean* and *mean absolute deviation (MAD).* Provide a dot plot with the following values: 2, 2, 3, 3, 4, 4, 4, 4, 5, 5, 6, 6. Ask, *How do we find the mean?* Prompt students to say **mean.** Model finding the mean (4), and then ask, *What is the mean?* Have students use a sentence frame: **The _____ is _____.** Repeat the process to review *mean absolute deviation.*	During the Check portion of the lesson, have students take turns echo reading the text. Start by reading through the entire problem one time. Then read it again, one sentence at a time, having students take turns echo reading each sentence after you. Be sure to read slowly and enunciate clearly. Provide feedback about correct pronunciation. As you guide students through solving the problem, have them continue echoing your explanations of each step.	On the board, display two dot plots with the following data: Plot 1: 15, 15, 16, 16, 16, 17, 17, 17, 18, 18; Plot 2: 17, 18, 18, 19, 19, 19, 19, 20, 20, 21. Then organize students in groups of four. Assign one student to be the "teacher." Have the three "students" assess the degree of visual overlap between the data sets. Each student will complete one step in the solving process before passing the paper on to the next student. When the problem has been solved, the "teacher" should review the work to ensure that it was correct and fix any errors. Then ask the "teachers" to present their group's work to the class.

Teacher Notes:

NAME _____ DATE _____ PERIOD _____

Lesson 5 Vocabulary
Assess Visual Overlap

Use the definition map to write a description and list characteristics about the vocabulary word or phrase. Write or draw math examples. Share your examples with a classmate.

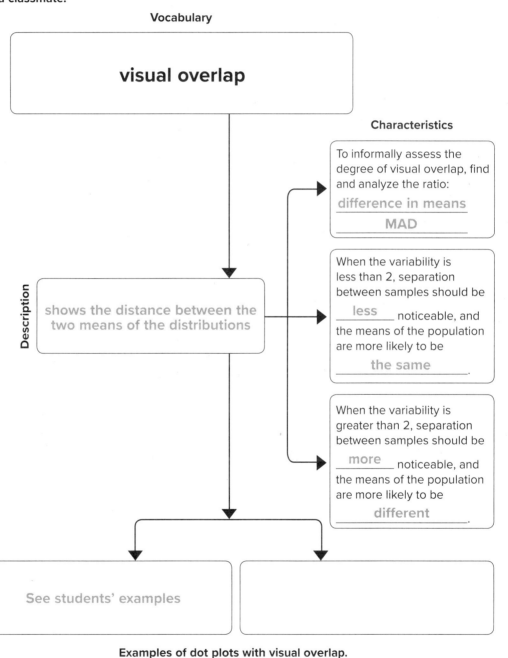

Vocabulary

visual overlap

Characteristics

To informally assess the degree of visual overlap, find and analyze the ratio:

$$\frac{\text{difference in means}}{\text{MAD}}$$

When the variability is less than 2, separation between samples should be _____ less _____ noticeable, and the means of the population are more likely to be _____ the same _____.

Description

shows the distance between the two means of the distributions

When the variability is greater than 2, separation between samples should be _____ more _____ noticeable, and the means of the population are more likely to be _____ different _____.

See students' examples

Examples of dot plots with visual overlap.

Lesson 1 Vertical and Adjacent Angles

English Learner Instructional Strategy

Sensory Support: Mnemonics

Write *congruent, adjacent angles, obtuse angle,* and *vertex* and their Spanish cognates, *congruente, ángulos adyacentes, ángulo obtuso,* and *vértice,* respectively. Introduce the words, and provide math examples. Use other translation tools for non-Spanish speaking ELLs. Add the words to a Word Wall.

Provide these mnemonics for types of angles: 1) Show a cyclist signaling a right turn, and compare the angle created by the cyclist's arm to a *right angle*. 2) Write: *The **acute** angle is a cute angle.* Discuss how *small* things are often described as *cute*. Then tell students acute angles are the *smallest* of the angles. 3) Write *obtuse* and exaggerate pronouncing its first syllable by opening your mouth wide and saying, *Ahhh-btuse*. Next, write and say, *Open **wide** to say **obtuse**.* Then tell students obtuse angles are *wider* than right angles and acute angles.

English Language Development Leveled Activities

Entering/Emerging	Developing/Expanding	Bridging
Choral Responses	**Building Oral Language**	**Synthesis**
Draw a ray that extends from an endpoint. Point to the endpoint and say, *This is an **endpoint**.* Have students repeat. Point to the ray and say, *This is a **ray**.* Have students repeat chorally. Then draw an angle. Point to each ray and say, *This is a **ray**.* Have students repeat. Then point to the vertex and say, *The rays have the **same** endpoint. It is called a **vertex**.* Have students repeat. Finally, trace the angle formed by the two rays, and say, *This is an **angle**.* Have students repeat. Randomly point to each part of the angle and have students name it chorally.	Review the definitions and examples for *right angle, acute angle, obtuse angle,* and *straight angle* from the lesson. Then use the hands of a demonstration clock to form different types of angles. Have students identify each one as a right angle, an acute angle, an obtuse, or a straight angle. Ask students to explain their responses using this sentence frame: **The angle is _____ because _____.**	Divide students into pairs, and distribute a demonstration clock to each pair. Have students use the clock to find four times: one at which the clock's hands form a right angle, one at which the hands form an acute angle, one at which the hands form an obtuse angle, and one at which the hands form a straight angle. Have them write each of the times. Then ask each pair to present their times and corresponding angles to an Entering/Emerging student.

Teacher Notes:

NAME _____ DATE _____ PERIOD _____

Lesson 1 Vocabulary

Vertical and Adjacent Angles

Use the three-column chart to write the vocabulary word and
definition for each drawing. Sample answers are given.

What I See	Vocabulary Word	Definition
	vertex	the common endpoint of the rays forming the angle
	right angle	an angle that measures exactly 90°
	acute angle	an angle with a measure greater than 0° and less than 90°
	obtuse angle	any angle that measures greater than 90 but less than 180°
	straight angle	an angle that measures exactly 180°
	vertical angles	opposite angles formed by the intersection of two lines
	congruent angles	angles that have the same measure
	adjacent angles	angles that have the same vertex, share a common side, and do not overlap

Module 11 *Geometric Figures*   **63**

Lesson 2 Complementary and Supplementary Angles

English Learner Instructional Strategy

Vocabulary Support: Cognates

Before the lesson, write *complementary angle* and *supplementary angle* and their Spanish cognates, *ángulos complementarios* and *ángulos suplementarios,* respectively, on a Word Wall. Introduce the words, and provide math examples. Utilize other translation tools for non-Spanish speaking ELLs. Discuss multiple meanings for *complementary* and *supplementary,* using pictures/demonstrations to support understanding. Finally, share this mnemonic for supplementary angles. Circle *supple* in *supplementary.* Explain how things described as *supple* are *flexible.* As an example, show a photo of a gymnast performing a split. Then show that the adjacent angles formed by his or her legs and torso are supplementary angles. (Note: The words *supple* and *supplementary* are not related in meaning.)

English Language Development Leveled Activities

Entering/Emerging	Developing/Expanding	Bridging
Word Knowledge	Developing Oral Language	Partner Work
Ensure students understand, that in this lesson, *adjacent* means "connected" rather than "near." Then point out examples. Say, *Our classroom is **adjacent to** [Teacher name]'s classroom. Our classrooms are **adjacent**. The classrooms share a common wall.* Next, draw several sets of angles, some adjacent and some not. Include complementary and supplementary angles among the adjacent angles. Then ask students to identify the angles in each set as **adjacent** or **not adjacent**. Finally, have them identify adjacent angles as **complementary** or **supplementary.**	Have students work with a partner to identify complementary and supplementary angles. Give pairs samples of adjacent angles, some that are complementary, some that are supplementary, and some that are neither. Ask one student to identify the angles as **complementary, supplementary,** or **neither** by sight, and have the other measure the angles and add their measurements to see if they equal 90° or 180°. Tell students to discuss what makes two angles complementary or supplementary.	Have each student create his or her own figure using intersecting lines. Tell students that their figure should include at least one pair of supplementary angles, one pair of complementary angles, and one pair of vertical angles. Have them label all the angles in their figure with a letter, and then exchange papers with a partner. Students should identify complementary, supplementary, and vertical angles in the figure they receive. Then have them check answers with the student who drew the figure.

Teacher Notes:

NAME _____ DATE _____ PERIOD _____

Lesson 2 Vocabulary

Complementary and Supplementary Angles

Use the word cards to define each vocabulary word or phrase and give an example. Sample answers are given.

Word Cards

complementary angles	ángulos complementarios
Definition	**Definición**
Two angles are complementary if the sum of their measures is 90°.	Dos ángulos son complementarios si la suma de sus medidas es 90°.

Example Sentence

Angle 1 and angle 2 add up to 90°. They are complementary angles.

Word Cards

supplementary angles	ángulos suplementarios
Definition	**Definición**
Two angles are supplementary if the sum of their measures is 180°.	Dos ángulos son suplementarios si la suma de sus medidas es 180°.

Example Sentence

Angle 1 and angle 2 add up to 180°. They are supplementary angles.

Lesson 3 Angle Relationships and Parallel Lines

English Learner Instructional Strategy

Graphic Support: Anchor Chart

Write *alternate exterior angles, alternate interior angles, corresponding angles, exterior angles, interior angles,* and *transversal* and their Spanish cognates, *ángulos alternos externos, ángulos alternos internos, ángulos correspondientes, ángulos externos, ángulos internos,* and *transversal,* on the Word Wall.

Create an anchor chart for the lesson vocabulary, including *parallel lines* and *perpendicular lines.* After drawing a set of parallel lines with a transversal on a large sheet of paper or poster board, have volunteers take turns adding definitions and labeling examples of lesson vocabulary on the chart.

English Language Development Leveled Activities

Entering/Emerging	Developing/Expanding	Bridging
Number Game	**Sentence Frames**	**Show What You Know**
Create a set of index cards that contain lesson vocabulary (one term per card). Give each student an erasable white board and have them each draw a set of parallel lines with a transversal. Have the first student choose a card. Say the word on the card, and have the student chorally repeat the word. Then say, *Show me ____.* Have the student draw an example of the vocabulary word on his or her white board. Assist the student as needed. Then ask the next student in line to choose a card. Repeat the activity until all students have had a turn, reshuffling the cards as needed.	Draw a set of parallel lines with a transversal. Label the angles and the lines. Then display the following sentence frames, and have students use them to describe the lines and angles: ____ **is parallel to** ____. ____ **is the transversal.** ____ **and** ____ **are corresponding angles.** ____ **and** ____ **are alternate [interior/ exterior] angles.** Then provide measurements for a couple of the angles, and ask, *If this angle's measurement is ____, what is the measure of angle ____?* Have students answer: ____ **degrees.**	Assign a problem involving using supplementary angles to solve for *x*. Have students work in pairs to solve it. Say, *List the steps you need to solve this problem.* Display the following sentence frames for students to use: **First ____. Then ____. Last ____.** After pairs have completed the task, have a couple of volunteers share what they wrote. Then have pairs exchange lists of steps. Display another similar problem with a pair of supplementary angles labeled, such as $6x°$ and $(x + 5)°$. Have pairs solve for *x* using the steps they were given.

Multicultural Teacher Tip

Encourage ELLs to share traditions, stories, songs, or other aspects of their native culture with the other students in class. You might even create a "culture wall" where all students can display cultural items. This will help create a classroom atmosphere of respect and appreciation for all cultures, and in turn, will create a more comfortable learning environment for ELLs.

NAME _____ DATE _____ PERIOD _____

Lesson 3 Vocabulary

Angle Relationships and Parallel Lines

Use the three-column chart to write the vocabulary word and definition
for each drawing. Sample answers are given.

What I See	Vocabulary Word	Definition
	perpendicular lines	two lines that intersect to form right angles
	parallel lines	Lines in the same plane that never intersect or cross; the symbol ‖ means parallel.
	transversal	a line that intersects two or more other lines
	interior angles	the four inside angles formed when two lines are cut by a transversal
	exterior angles	the four outer angles formed when two lines are cut by a transversal
	alternate interior angles	interior angles that lie on opposite sides of the transversal
	alternate exterior angles	exterior angles that lie on opposite sides of the transversal
	corresponding angles	angles that are in the same position on two lines in relation to a transversal

Module 11 *Geometric Figures* **65**

Lesson 4 Triangles

English Learner Instructional Strategy

Language Structure Support: Choral Responses

Write *acute triangle, equilateral triangle, isosceles triangle, scalene triangle,* and *congruent segments,* and their Spanish cognates, *triángulo acutángulo, triángulo equilátero, triángulo isosceles, triángulo escaleno,* and *segmentos congruentes,* respectively. Introduce the words, and provide math examples. Utilize other translation tools for non-Spanish speaking ELLs. Add the words to a Word Wall.

After the lesson, revisit types of triangles by drawing an example of each on the board. Include a right triangle and an obtuse triangle, in addition to those already named in this activity. Then point to each triangle and ask, for example, *Is this an **isosceles** triangle or an **obtuse** triangle?* Have students chorally say the name of the triangle.

English Language Development Leveled Activities

Entering/Emerging	Developing/Expanding	Bridging
Word Recognition	**Word Identification**	**Anchor Chart**
Give students pictures of objects or scenes that have triangles in them. The pictures may be printed, photocopied, or torn from a newspaper or magazine. Tell students to trace the outline of each triangle they find in a picture. Then have them label each triangle, using one or more of these names, as appropriate: *acute triangle, obtuse triangle, right triangle, scalene triangle, isosceles triangle,* or *equilateral triangle.* Show students that all triangles can be labeled correctly with more than one name. Have students show their labeled pictures to the class.	Have students make flashcards for the different types of triangles described in this lesson. On one side of the card, tell them to write the term. On the other side, have them write a definition and then draw and label an example. Encourage students to include terms/cognates from their native language to help describe the triangles on the flashcards. When cards are completed, have students work in pairs to quiz each other using the flashcards. Encourage students to create a pocket in their math notebook to store the cards for future reference.	Tell students that many triangles have common features. Have partners work together to answer these questions about the triangles from this lesson: *Which triangles always have all acute angles?* **acute triangle, equilateral triangle** *Which triangles have no congruent sides?* **scalene triangles** *Which triangles always have at least two congruent sides?* **isosceles triangle, equilateral triangle** *After partners have answered the questions, ask them to make a chart that summarizes their findings.*

Teacher Notes:

NAME _____ DATE _____ PERIOD _____

Lesson 4 Vocabulary

Triangles

Use the three-column chart to write the vocabulary word and definition for each drawing. Sample answers are given.

What I See	Vocabulary Word	Definition
Name by **angles**	acute triangle	a triangle with three acute angles
	right triangle	a triangle with one right angle
	obtuse triangle	a triangle with one obtuse angle
Name by **sides**	scalene triangle	a triangle with no congruent sides
	isosceles triangle	a triangle with at least two congruent sides
	equilateral triangle	a triangle with three congruent sides
General vocabulary	triangle	a figure with three sides and three angles
	congruent segments	sides that are the same length

Lesson 5 Angle Relationships and Triangles

English Learner Instructional Strategy

Sensory Support: Manipulatives

Write *triangle* and its Spanish cognate, *triángulo,* on the Word Wall, along with examples of different kinds of triangles to provide concrete examples. As students refer to *triangles* and *angles* during the lesson, listen for the final /z/ sound indicating plural. If the final *s* is being said as /s/, model the correct pronunciation and have students repeat.

Divide students into four groups. Distribute a different triangle to each group, along with a protractor. Have students trace their triangles onto paper. Say, *Use the protractor to measure two angles of your triangle. Write each measurement by the angle. For the third angle, write x.* Have groups exchange papers. Then say, *Find the value of* x *in the triangle you were given.* Display sentence frames for students to use in sharing their answers: **The given angles' measures are _____. The value of** *x* **is _____.** Be sure students are differentiating between *are* and *is* correctly to demonstrate understanding of singular and plural verbs.

English Language Development Leveled Activities

Entering/Emerging	Developing/Expanding	Bridging
Word Knowledge	Academic Word Knowledge	Communication Guide
Write *remote* in a word web. Fill in the rest of the web with synonyms for *remote,* such as *far, distant, not close, not nearby.* Display a triangle with a side extended and the exterior angle and interior angles labeled *a, b, c,* and *d.* Indicate the exterior angle, and then point to the remote angles as you say, *These angles are farther away. They are the remote angles.* Then create a two-column chart labeled *Interior* and *Exterior.* Fill the chart with student examples of objects found inside and outside a building or home.	Create several three-card sets with the following math vocabulary: *interior angle, exterior angle, remote interior angles.* Randomly distribute one card to each student. Have students get into groups of three based on the card sets, and give each group a protractor. Say, *Draw a triangle. Extend one side. Use the protractor to measure the angles.* Then ask each student to say the measurement of the angle or angles referred to on the card. Display the following sentence frames: **The measure of _____ angle is _____ degrees. The measure of _____ angles are _____ and _____.**	Have students work in small groups to create guides for classifying triangles. Each page should feature one type of triangle, including its name, a sentence describing it, and a visual example and non-example. List the following types of triangles: *obtuse, acute, right, equilateral, isosceles,* and *scalene.* Provide the following sentence frames for students to use: **A _____ triangle has _____. The sum of the angle measures in this triangle is _____.** Add the guides to a student reference library so they are available for future use.

Teacher Notes:

NAME _____ DATE _____ PERIOD _____

Lesson 5 Vocabulary

Angle Relationships and Triangles

Use the vocabulary squares to write a definition and a sentence. Then label the
figure with an example for each vocabulary word. Sample answers are given.

	Definition
interior angle	the angle formed by the segments that lie inside the triangle
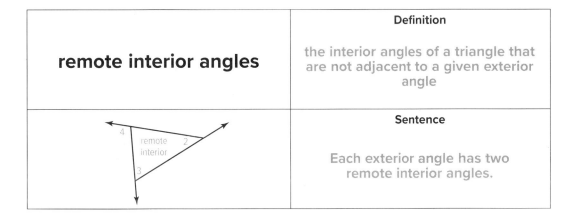	**Sentence** A triangle has three interior angles.

	Definition
exterior angle	the angle formed by one side of the triangle and the extension of the adjacent side
	Sentence A triangle has three exterior angle.

	Definition
remote interior angles	the interior angles of a triangle that are not adjacent to a given exterior angle
	Sentence Each exterior angle has two remote interior angles.

Module 11 *Geometric Figures*   **67**

Lesson 6 Scale Drawings

English Learner Instructional Strategy

Sensory Support: Illustrations, Diagrams, and Drawings

Before the lesson, write *scale model* and *scale factor* and their Spanish cognates, *modelo a escala* and *factor de escala,* respectively. Introduce the words, and provide math examples to support understanding. Utilize other appropriate translation tools for non-Spanish speaking ELLs. Add the words to a Word Wall.

During the lesson, show students an assortment of maps, and point out the scale on each. Use the scales to estimate the number of miles or kilometers between cities, states, and countries. Also, show students other examples of scale models and drawings, such as floor plan samples from home improvement magazines, architect's blue prints, and needlework guides.

English Language Development Leveled Activities

Entering/Emerging	Developing/Expanding	Bridging
Listen and Write	**Look, Listen, and Identify**	**Partner Work**
Show and explain what a statue is and who Thomas Jefferson was. Then write this problem: *Thomas Jefferson was x feet tall. A statue of him is 19 feet tall. The scale for the statue is 3 feet = 1 foot. What is the value of x?* Write and say the reworded problem. Then have partners work together to write and solve an expression to find Thomas Jefferson's height.	Write and say the following word problem: *Ted is making a scale drawing of a kitchen. The kitchen measures 9 feet by 12 feet. The scale for the drawing is 1 inch equals 3 feet.* Have students use the scale to draw the kitchen on 1-inch grid paper. Then have them answer these questions: *What are the actual dimensions of the scale drawing?* **3 inches by 4 inches** *Will the scale drawing by larger or smaller than the actual kitchen?* **smaller**	Have partners measure the dimensions of the classroom and round the measurements to the nearest foot. Then have students make a scale drawing of the room. Tell them to choose a scale, keeping in mind that their drawings will need to fit on a piece of grid paper. Then have them make their drawings. Each student should work individually and then compare papers with his or her partner. Have partners note how their drawings are alike and different. Discuss as a class why the sizes of drawings may differ but their shapes should not.

Teacher Notes:

NAME _____ DATE _____ PERIOD _____

Lesson 6 Vocabulary

Scale Drawings

Use the vocabulary squares to write a definition, a sentence, and an example for each vocabulary word. Sample answers are given.

scale drawing	**Definition**
	a drawing that is used to represent objects that are too large or too small to be drawn at actual size
Example	**Sentence**
	A scale drawing was used to show the furniture placement in the room.

scale model	**Definition**
	a model used to represent objects that are too large or too small to be built at actual size
Example	**Sentence**
	A scale model was used to represent the 15 story building.

scale factor	**Definition**
	a scale written as ratio without units in simplest form
Example	**Sentence**
$\frac{1}{18}$	The scale of a model is 1 in. = 1.5 feet. The scale factor is $\frac{1}{18}$.

Lesson 7 Three-Dimensional Figures

English Learner Instructional Strategy

Vocabulary Support: Cognates

Before the lesson, write *prism, base, pyramid, plane, coplanar, cylinder,* and *cone,* and their Spanish cognates, *prisma, base, pirámide, plano, coplanar, cilindro,* and *cono,* respectively. Introduce the words, and provide math examples. Utilize other translation tools for non-Spanish speaking ELLs. Add the words to a Word Wall.

Discuss multiple meanings for these words: *prism, base, plane, cone.* Use real-world objects, photos, and demonstrations to support understanding. Finally, tell students that these words are homophones: *base/bass, plane/plain.* Discuss multiple meanings for *bass* and *plain.*

English Language Development Leveled Activities

Entering/Emerging	Developing/Expanding	Bridging
Anchor Chart	**Word Identification**	**Word Knowledge**
Draw and label the vertices of a large rectangular prism and a large triangular prism. Ask volunteers to come to the board and identify an edge, a face, a base, and a vertex on each prism. If students are having difficulty, help them start an anchor chart for three-dimensional figures that includes the name of each figure and a diagram showing what the figure looks like with its parts labeled.	Have students make flashcards for the vocabulary words in this lesson. Write and discuss these guidelines: *1) On one side of the card, write the term. 2) On the other side of the card, write a definition. Include a drawing.* Encourage students to use words/cognates from their native language to help define and describe the terms on the flashcards. After they have had time to work, have partners quiz each using their flashcards.	Have partners make a list of vocabulary words and other terms introduced in this lesson. Then have them use a dictionary to determine which terms have multiple meanings. Remind students that some vocabulary words with multiple meanings were discussed before the lesson. Others that students should address include *face, edge,* and *vertex.* Have students discuss how the meanings for each word differ and whether or not the various meanings seem to be related at all. Have students make a table to organize their findings. Then invite them to present their tables to the class.

Teacher Notes:

NAME _____ DATE _____ PERIOD _____

Lesson 7 Vocabulary

Three-Dimensional Figures

Use the three-column chart to organize the vocabulary in this lesson. Write the
word in Spanish. Then write the definition of each word. Sample answers are given.

English	Spanish	Definition
polyhedron	poliedro	three-dimensional figure, or solid, with flat surfaces that are polygons
prism	prisma	a 3D figure with at least three rectangular lateral faces and top and bottom faces are parallel
base	base	In a prism, the pair of parallel, congruent faces. In a pyramid, the polygon containing the base edge of the, lateral, triangular faces.
pyramid	pirámide	a 3D figure with at least three lateral faces that are triangles and only one base
face	cara	a flat surface of a polyhedron
edge	borde	the line segment where two faces of the polyhedron intersect
vertex	vértice	the point where three or more planes intersect
cylinder	cilindro	a 3D figure with two parallel congruent circular bases connected by a curved surface
cone	cono	a 3D figure one circular base connected by a curved side to a single point

Lesson 1 Circumference of Circles

English Learner Instructional Strategy

Vocabulary Support: Word Knowledge

Before the lesson, write *radius, center,* and *pi* and their Spanish cognates, *radio, centro,* and *pi,* respectively. Introduce the words, and provide math examples. Utilize other translation tools for non-Spanish speaking ELLs. Then discuss these word features: 1) *Radius* contains the root word *rad,* meaning "ray." Help students relate the meaning of *ray* to the meaning of *radius.* 2) Pronounce *center,* emphasizing the /s/ at the beginning of the word. Then give students this tip for remembering the pronunciation: *c* followed by *e* or *i* usually makes this sound in English: /s/. Invite other examples of words with /s/ spelled *ce* or *ci.* **Sample response: <u>c</u>ir<u>c</u>umferen<u>ce</u>** 3) Pronounce *pi* and then tell students that this word is a homophone of *pie.* Use a photo or illustration to help you define *pie.*

Add the words and their cognates to a Word Wall along with math examples.

English Language Development Leveled Activities

Entering/Emerging	Developing/Expanding	Bridging
Anchor Chart	**Number Game**	**Share What You Know**
Distribute these materials to groups of students: scissors, glue, construction paper, poster board, string, an adhesive dot, drinking straws. Have each group cut a different sized circle from the construction paper and then mount it on poster board. Next have students attach the following to their circles: a center point made with the dot, a radius and a diameter cut from straws, and a circumference made of string. Have groups label each part of their completed model with the correct vocabulary term and definition. Compile students' work onto an anchor chart and post for students to use as a reference.	Give partners a number cube, a compass, a ruler, and a piece of string. Then discuss these game rules: *1) One student rolls the number cube. The number rolled is a circle's radius in inches. Use the compass to draw a circle with that radius. 2) The other student uses the string and ruler to measure the circle's circumference. Then he or she uses the formula $C = \pi d$ to find the circumference of the circle. Record both circumference measurements and compare them. Are they similar? 3) Partners switch roles to play the next round.* Have students play a few rounds.	Divide students into pairs and tell them they will be working together on a research project about how different cultures use circles in art. Share examples of circle art, such as "eternity" bands and Native American dream catchers. Then ask pairs to choose a type of circle art to research. If students need ideas, you might suggest the Olympic rings, flag art, mandalas, or even the "circle of life" diagrams found in science textbooks. Have pairs create a poster showing examples of their chosen art, notes about its meaning, and the history of its use. Then ask them to share their posters with the class.

Teacher Notes:

NAME _____ DATE _____ PERIOD _____

Lesson 1 Vocabulary
Circumference of Circles

Use the three column chart to write the vocabulary word and definition for each drawing. Sample answers are given.

What I See	Vocabulary Word	Definition
	circle	the set of all points in a plane that are the same distance from a given point called the center
	center	the point from which all points on circle are the same distance
	circumference	the distance around a circle
	diameter	the distance across a circle through its center
	radius	the distance from the center of a circle to any point on the circle
π	pi	the ratio of the circumference of a circle to its diameter

Lesson 2 Area of Circles

English Learner Instructional Strategy

Sensory Support: Mnemonics

Before the lesson, write *semicircle* and its Spanish cognate, *semicirculo*. Introduce the word, and show an example. Utilize other translation tools for non-Spanish speaking ELLs. Then underline *semi* and tell students these letters form a prefix that means "half." Help students use the meaning of *semi-* to define *semicircle* as "a half circle." Then show students how two semicircles put together form a full circle.

Draw the sign ($\approx$) for "approximately equals." Help students remember its meaning by showing its likeness to the equals sign and to ocean waves. Discuss how, like waves show a surface isn't perfectly flat, the "approximately equals" sign shows an equation isn't perfectly precise.

English Language Development Leveled Activities

Entering/Emerging	Developing/Expanding	Bridging
Word Knowledge	Share What You Know	Show What You Know
Differentiate math meanings for *square*. Say, *A square is a* **figure**. Show students pictures of geometric figures, identifying each. Then say, *A square is a* **measurement**. Use a ruler to draw a 3-inch line. Say, *This measurement is 3 inches.* Then draw a rectangle that is 3 inches in width and 1 inch in height. Say, *This measurement is 3* **square** *inches*. Show how the measurement includes the area of each unit. Finally, say, *I can* **square** *a number.* Write and discuss: the **square** of 3; 3 **squared** = 3 × 3 or 3².	Give each student a different-sized circle. Circles may be drawn and cut out, or they may be classroom objects. Ask students to write step-by-step instructions for applying the formula for area to their circles. Have them use this guide: **Start with this formula: _____. Then, measure the circle's _____. My circle's _____ measures _____ [units]. Use the measurement in place of this part of the formula: _____. Then, multiply. The area of my circle is _____ square [units].**	Ask, *What are two formulas for finding the circumference of a circle?* Invite volunteers to come to the board and write one of the formulas. **A = 3.14r^2, A = $\frac{22}{7}r^2$** Then point to the one that uses a fraction. Ask, *When and why should we use this formula?* Have students write their explanations in their notebooks. Then invite volunteers to share their explanations with the class.

Multicultural Teacher Tip

Mathematical notation varies from culture to culture, so you may find ELLs using unfamiliar symbols in place of standard U.S. symbols. For example, students from Latin American countries may use a point in place of × to show multiplication. Although the point is also commonly used in the US, the placement and size may vary depending on the native culture. In Mexico, the point is larger and set higher between the numbers than in the U.S. In some Latin American countries, the point is set low and can be confused with a decimal point.

NAME _____ DATE _____ PERIOD _____

Lesson 2 Vocabulary
Area of Circles

Use the definition map to list qualities about the vocabulary word or phrase.
Sample answers are given.

Vocabulary

semicircle

Description

half of a circle

Characteristics

$A = \frac{1}{2}\pi r^2$

The area of a
semicircle is half the
area of a circle with the
same radius.

Draw examples of semicircles.

Module 12 *Area, Surface Area, and Volume* **71**

Lesson 3 Area of Composite Figures

English Learner Instructional Strategy

Sensory Support: Realia, Photographs, and Physical Activities

Write *composite figure* and its Spanish cognate, *figura compuesto* on the Word Wall. Introduce the term, and provide a math example. Utilize other translation tools for non-Spanish speaking ELLs.

Then show the meanings of these terms from the problems on the student pages: ***flag***, *non-rectangular*, *burgee*, *swallowtail*, *reclaimed*, ***painting***; *community center*, *ceramic tile*, *mosaic*, ***counter***, *countertop*. (Note: Boldface terms are multiple-meaning words.)

English Language Development Leveled Activities

Entering/Emerging	Developing/Expanding	Bridging
Listen and Identify Collect a variety of pictures that show these figures: trapezoid, triangle, circle, rectangle, square, pentagon, hexagon, octagon. The figure may be represented by an object, it may be the focal point of a piece of art or architecture, it may be from nature, or it may be hand drawn. Distribute a few pictures to each student and have them identify the focal figure in each. Then call out each figure name. Have students repeat the name chorally and then hold up a picture, if they have one that shows the figure. Encourage students to identify features that help them classify the figure.	**Anchor Chart** Assign each student one of these figures: parallelogram, rectangle, semicircle, square, triangle, trapezoid. Tell students to create an anchor chart for their figure that includes its name, a list of the figure's key features, pictures of the figure, non-examples of the figure, and the formula to find the area of the figure. Display each anchor chart and encourage students to use it as a reference.	**Public Speaking Norms** Have each student draw a composite figure, using whatever shapes he or she wants. Then ask students to exchange drawings with a partner. Have the partner identify the shapes within the composite and then take the measurements needed to calculate its area. Finally, have students present the composite figures they received to the class. Tell them their presentations should include an explanation of how they determined the area of the composite figure.

Teacher Notes:

NAME _____ DATE _____ PERIOD _____

Lesson 3 Notetaking

Area of Composite Figures

Use Cornell notes to better understand the lesson's concepts. Complete each sentence by filling in the blanks with the correct word or phrase.

Questions	Notes
1. How do I find the area of a composite figure?	Since a composite figure is made up of two or more ___shapes___ , decompose the composite figure. Decompose it into shapes with known ___area___ formulas. Then find the ___sum___ of these ___areas___ .
2. How do I find the area of a shaded region?	Use shapes with ___area formulas___ that are known. For example, find the area of a region larger than the shaded region and ___subtract___ the non-shaded regions.

Summary
How do measurements help you describe real-world objects? See students' work.

Lesson 4 Volume of Prisms and Pyramids

English Learner Instructional Strategy

Collaborative Support: Numbered Heads Together

Organize students into four groups. Give each student in the group a number from one to four. Have groups work together to solve the problems in the lesson. For each problem, tell them to agree on a solution and ensure everyone in their group understands and can give an answer. Work through the problems with students. For each item, call out a number (1–4) randomly. The students assigned to that number should raise their hands and, when called on, answer for their team.

English Language Development Leveled Activities

Entering/Emerging	Developing/Expanding	Bridging
Phonemic Awareness	**Word Knowledge**	**Public Speaking Norms**
Write *face* on the board and pronounce it with students. Take care in enunciating the initial /f/, a sound that does not transfer from all languages. If students need help, show them they can make the sound by biting their lower lip and blowing lightly. Then discuss meanings for *face*. Show students that, within the context of this lesson, a *face* is a side of an object that is on the *outside* of the object. Demonstrate using a paper box. Point to different sides of the box saying, *This is a* **face**. *It is on the* **outside**. Then point to its inside surfaces saying, *This is* **not** *a face. It is on the* **inside**.	Write *face* on the board and pronounce it with students. Remind them that *c* followed by *e* makes this sound: /s/. Then show students that, within the context of this lesson, a *face* is a side on the *outside* of the object. Demonstrate this meaning as shown in the Entering/Emerging Level activity. Then write and say *lateral*. Explain and show that something described as *lateral* appears on the *side* of an object, as opposed to its top or bottom. Now, show students two photos, one of a climber at the top of a mountain and one of a climber scaling a cliff. Ask, *Which climber is on a lateral face?* **the climber on the cliff**	Have students write real-world problems of their own. Then have students exchange papers with a partner. Have the partner solve the problem he or she received and then share the problem and solution with the class.

Teacher Notes:

NAME _____ DATE _____ PERIOD _____

Lesson 4 Vocabulary

Volume of Prisms and Pyramids

Use the flow chart to review the processes for finding the volume of a prism or pyramid. Sample answers are given.

Volume
Define volume.

the number of cubic units needed to fill

the space occupied by a solid

Determine the type of three-dimensional object.

Prism
Define prism.

a polyhedron with two

parallel and congruent

faces called bases

Pyramid
Define pyramid.

A polyhedron with a base that

is a polygon and three or more

triangular faces that meet in a

common vertex

Write the formula to find the
volume of a prism.

$V = Bh$

Write the formula to find the volume
of a pyramid.

$V = \frac{1}{3} Bh$

Module 12 *Area, Surface Area, and Volume*   **73**

Lesson 5 Surface Area of Prisms and Pyramids

English Learner Instructional Strategy

Vocabulary Support: Make Connections

Before the lesson, write *surface area* and its Spanish cognate, *área de superficie* on the Word Wall. Introduce the term, and provide a math example. Utilize other translation tools for non-Spanish speaking ELLs. Then discuss multiple meanings for *surface*. Help students understand that, within the context of this lesson, *surface* is an adjective. However, *surface* also has noun and verb meanings. For example, noun meanings of *surface* include "the outside layer of something" and "information that has become public," and verb meanings include "to appear or become visible" and "to cover a surface with a coat of something, such as asphalt." Discuss with students how all these meanings for surface are related. Guide students to understand that all have to do with the *outside* of something, or the part of something that people can easily see or know.

English Language Development Leveled Activities

Entering/Emerging	Developing/Expanding	Bridging
Read and Write	**Sentence Frames**	**Number Game**
Write the following problem on the board: *Make a rectangular prism. The dimensions must be whole numbers. The maximum surface area is 160 square feet. Maximize the volume in your prism.* Ask, *What kind of prism is it? Is it* **rectangular** *or* **triangular**? **rectangular** Then say, *Here are the rules. 1) Use whole numbers. 2) Use the greatest volume possible. 3) Use the least surface area possible. 4) The maximum surface area is 160 square feet.* Show the meanings of *greatest, least,* and *maximum.* Then work through the problem with students.	Write the following dimensions: length = 9 inches, width = 6 inches, and height = 3 inches. Then say, *These are the dimensions for a rectangular prism.* Have students draw a model of the prism and label its length, width, and height. Then have them write step-by-step instructions for calculating its surface area. Provide these sentence frames for students to use: **This formula shows the area of the prism's top and bottom: ____. This formula shows the area of the prism's front and back: ____. This formula shows the area of the prism's other two sides: ____. The sum of the areas is ____ square inches.**	Organize students into pairs, and give each pair a number cube. Then discuss these game rules: *1) One student rolls the number cube 3 times. The numbers rolled are the dimensions for a rectangular prism. The first number is its length, the second number is its width, and the third number is its height. The student draws the prism and calculates its surface area. 2) The other student takes a turn, repeating the steps in Rule 1. 3) Partners compare surface areas. The student with the greater surface area scores one point. 4) Partners continue taking turns until one student has five points.*

Teacher Notes:

NAME _____ DATE _____ PERIOD _____

Lesson 5 Vocabulary

Surface Area of Prisms and Pyramids

Use the vocabulary squares to write a definition and a sentence for each
vocabulary word. Sample answers are given.

surface area of a prism	Definition
	the sum of the areas of all of the faces of a prism
Write the formula for a rectangular prism. S.A. $= 2\ell h + 2\ell w + 2hw$	**Draw a Figure** 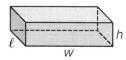

slant height of a pyramid	Definition
	the height of each lateral face
Draw an arrow showing the slant height. 	**Sentence** The slant height is used to find the surface area of a lateral face of a pyramid.

surface area of a pyramid	Definition
	the sum of all of the faces of a pyramid
Write the formula for a square pyramid. S.A. $= s^2 + 4\left(\frac{1}{2}bh\right)$	**Draw a Figure** 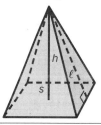

Lesson 6 Volume of Cylinders

English Learner Instructional Strategy

Collaborative Support: Round the Table

Write *volume* and *cylinder* and their Spanish cognates, *volumen* and *cilindro,* on the Word Wall. Briefly introduce the meaning of each word, and then, during the lesson, frequently refer to the Word Wall to reinforce meaning and to provide concrete examples for each term.

Place students into multilingual groups of 4, and write the following problem on the board: *To the nearest tenth, find the volume of a cylinder with a height of 1.8 in. and a radius of 3 in.* Have one student draw a model of the problem on a large piece of paper. Then have the other students work to solve the problem by passing the paper around the table. Each student will perform one step in a different color pen to find the volume. Afterward, choose one student to present the solution to the class. Repeat with another example.

English Language Development Leveled Activities

Entering/Emerging	Developing/Expanding	Bridging
Word Knowledge Use an empty container to model volume as capacity. Then fill the container with rice or some other small objects. Say, *Volume is the amount of space inside.* Say *volume* again and have students chorally repeat. Display several clear containers. Work with students to order them from least to greatest volume. Ask either/or questions, such as: *Does this one hold more or less than that one?*	**Anchor Charts** Divide students into four groups. Say, *Choose a real-world example of something shaped like a cylinder. Then make an anchor chart showing how to find the volume of the cylinder.* Each chart should include a title at the top and a labeled example of the cylinder. When the charts are completed, have groups display and describe their charts. Display the following sentence frames for students to use: **Our cylinder is a(n) _____. [name of object] The volume is _____.**	**Show What You Know** Have students work in small groups. Have each group locate an example of a cylinder in the classroom. Give each group a metric ruler, and have them measure the object to determine the radius of its base and its height/length, rounded to the nearest millimeter. Say, *Use the measurements to determine the cylinder's volume.* Afterward, have a volunteer from each group share the measurement using the sentence frame: **The volume of the _____ is _____ cubic millimeters.**

Multicultural Teacher Tip

You may find ELLs write numbers using slightly different notations. In some countries, the groups may be separated by points (3.252.689) or spaces (3 252 689), and in Mexico it may be a combination of a comma and apostrophe (3'252,689) or a comma and semicolon (3;252,689). Similarly, some countries use a comma (3,45) to write decimals instead of a decimal point.

NAME _____ DATE _____ PERIOD _____

Lesson 6 Vocabulary

Volume of Cylinders

Use the vocabulary squares to write a definition, a sentence, and an example for each vocabulary word. Sample answers are given.

volume	**Definition**
	the measure of the space occupied by a solid; standard measures are cubic units such as in^3 or ft^3

Example	**Sentence**
$V = Bh$ $B = \pi r^2$ $V = Bh$	The volume of a cylinder is the area of the base multiplied by the height of the cylinder.

cylinder	**Definition**
	a three-dimensional figure with two parallel congruent circular bases connected by a curved surface

Draw a cylinder.	**Sentence**
	A real world example of a cylinder is a can of soup.

Lesson 7 Volume of Cones

English Learner Instructional Strategy

Vocabulary Support: Sentence Frames

Write *cone* and its Spanish cognate, *cono,* on the Word Wall. Provide a concrete example by displaying a cone manipulative or an example of a cone-shaped object in the classroom.

Display the following sentence frames to help students participate during the lesson:

Entering/Emerging: **The radius is _____. The height is _____. The volume is _____.**

Developing/Expanding: **If the diameter is _____, then the radius is _____. First we need to _____.**

Bridging: **I know the figure is a cone because _____.**

English Language Development Leveled Activities

Entering/Emerging	Developing/Expanding	Bridging
Academic Vocabulary	**Building Oral Language**	**Academic Word Knowledge**
Have students get into small groups and use translation tools to review any unknown vocabulary in the lesson. Have students write definitions for the terms in their notebooks and draw examples. Allow students to write the definitions in their own words and/or in their native languages. Afterward, regroup students and have them share what they wrote with the students in the new group.	Divide students into pairs. Have each pair draw a model of a cone. Say, *Label the radius and height, and provide measurements for both.* Give pairs time to complete the task, and then have them exchange drawings with another pair. Say, *Find the volume of the cone.* Then write the formula for the volume of a cone: $V = \frac{1}{3}\pi r^2 h$. Have one student from each pair read the formula aloud using the measurements of the cone: **The volume is one-third times pi times _____ squared times _____. The volume is _____ square _____.**	Have each student draw a cone with the measurements of the radius and height labeled. Have students use the formula for finding the volume of a cone to determine the volume of the cone they drew. Several volunteers can verbally describe how they used the formula to find the volume. Gather students' drawings and put them together in a classroom portfolio that can be used for future reference or display them in the classroom.

Teacher Notes:

NAME _____ DATE _____ PERIOD _____

Lesson 7 Vocabulary
Volume of Cones

Use the word cards to define each vocabulary word or phrase and give an example. Sample answers are given.

Word Cards

cone	cono
Definition	**Definición**
a three-dimensional figure with	una figura tridimensional con una
one circular base connected by	circular base conectada por una
a curved surface to a vertex	superficie curva para un vértice

Example Sentence

Sometimes, a party hat is cone shaped.

_____

Word Cards

vertex	vértice
Definition	**Definición**
the point at the tip of a cone	el punto en la punta de un
	cono

Example Sentence

Every cone has exactly one vertex.

_____

Lesson 8 Volume of Spheres

English Learner Instructional Strategy

Collaborative Support: Numbered Heads Together

Write *sphere* and *hemisphere* and their Spanish cognates, *esfera* and *hemisferio*, on the Word Wall. Provide concrete examples for *sphere* by locating spherical objects in the classroom or by having students brainstorm a list, such as *ball, globe, marble, bubble,* and so on. For *hemisphere,* identify the Northern and Southern Hemispheres on a globe and relate the geographical meaning to the math meaning.

Organize students into multilingual groups of four and number students as 1–4. Assign a problem to each group. They should discuss the problem, agree on a solution, and ensure that everyone in the group understands and can give the answer. Afterward, call out a random number from 1 to 4. Have students assigned to that number raise their hands and answer for their team.

English Language Development Leveled Activities

Entering/Emerging	Developing/Expanding	Bridging
Exploring Language Structure	**Report Back**	**Listen, Write, and Read**
Write *sphere* and *hemisphere*. Underline the *ph* in each word. Slowly and clearly model pronunciation of each word, pointing to the *ph* as you say that word part. Write *ph = f* and provide some additional examples of words with *ph,* such as *graph, telephone, Phoenix, photo.* Say each word, emphasizing the /f/. Have students chorally repeat.	Write the following problem: *A ball has a diameter of 8 inches. It has a slow leak. Air is escaping at the rate of 2.5 cubic inches per second. How long would it take the ball to deflate? Round to the nearest tenth.* Have students work in pairs to solve. Display the following order words on the board: *first, second, then, next, last, finally.* Say, *As you solve, write a sentence describing each step. Use order words in your sentences.* After students complete the solution, have one student from each pair read the sentences they wrote. Provide a sentence frame for students to use when reporting the solution: **The ball would deflate in about _____ seconds.**	Have students get into small groups. Ask, *If you know the volume of a hemisphere, how would you find the volume of a sphere with an equal diameter?* Give groups time to discuss the question, and then have each student write a sentence or two describing the group's answer. Come together again as a single group, and say, *Exchange papers with another student.* Have students proofread for any errors in spelling, grammar, or punctuation, and then return the papers to their authors. Ask a few volunteers to read their answers.

Teacher Notes:

NAME _____ DATE _____ PERIOD _____

Lesson 8 Vocabulary
Volume of Spheres

Use the definition map to list qualities about the vocabulary word or phrase.
Sample answers are given.

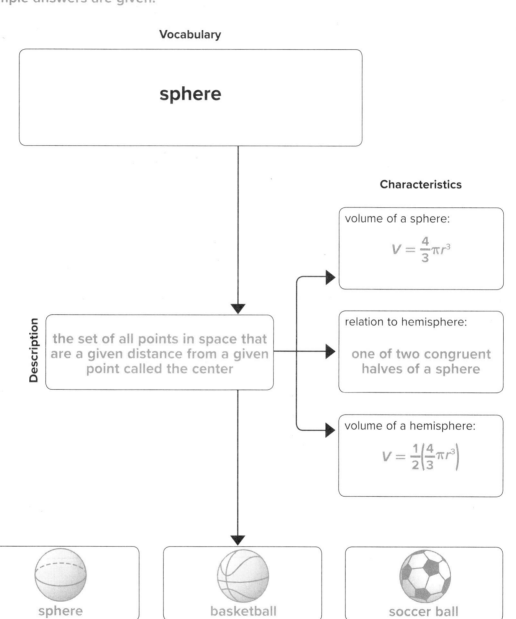

Vocabulary

sphere

Characteristics

volume of a sphere:

$$V = \frac{4}{3}\pi r^3$$

Description

the set of all points in space that are a given distance from a given point called the center

relation to hemisphere:

one of two congruent halves of a sphere

volume of a hemisphere:

$$V = \frac{1}{2}\left(\frac{4}{3}\pi r^3\right)$$

sphere

basketball

soccer ball

Draw and label three examples of spheres.

Module 12 *Area, Surface Area, and Volume* **77**

Lesson 9 Volume and Surface Area of Composite Solids

English Learner Instructional Strategy

Collaborative Support: Graffiti Poster

Ask students: *How can you find the **surface area** of a three-dimensional composite solid? How can you find its **volume**?* Have students create a graffiti poster and list their ideas about the answers to the questions. Have them include drawings and figures as well. Then have students turn and talk to a neighbor about their ideas. After students have had time to discuss, ask them to share with the class. As students share, make notes on the graffiti poster. Then tell students they will continue working with three-dimensional composite solids in this lesson.

English Language Development Leveled Activity

Entering/Emerging	Developing/Expanding	Bridging
Look, Listen, and Identify	Think-Pair-Share	Cooperative Learning
Present models of several different composite solids to students. Point to each face on a solid and ask, *Does this face have one shape or two shapes?* Have students hold up an index finger if the face has one simple shape, and have them hold up two fingers if the face was made with two simple shapes (such as a triangle on top of a square). Then have students name the shape(s) of each face.	Present models of several different composite solids to students. Have students identify the faces of each solid and then tell you the formula they would use to find the area of each face. To extend the activity, have students measure the faces of the solid. Then have them discuss each step for calculating its total surface area with a partner. Finally, ask students to "coach" you through finding the total surface area.	Divide students into three groups, and assign each group a problem involving three-dimensional composite solids. Have the students in each group work together to: 1) identify the solids used to form each composite solid; 2) decide how to calculate each solid's volume or surface area; and then 3) solve the problem. Once groups have completed their work, have each group present their problem to the other groups. Ask audience members to check the presenting group's calculations and make sure they agree the calculations are correct.

Teacher Notes:

NAME _____ DATE _____ PERIOD _____

Lesson 9 Notetaking

Volume and Surface Area of Composite Solids

Use Cornell notes to better understand the lesson's concepts. Complete each
sentence by filling in the blanks with the correct word or phrase.

Questions	Notes
1. How do I find the volume of a composite solid?	Since a composite solid is made up of two or more ____three-dimensional solids____ , decompose the composite solid. Separate it into solids whose ____volume____ formulas are known. Then find the ____sum____ of these ____volumes____ .
2. How do I find the surface area of a composite solid?	Find the ____areas____ of the ____faces____ that make up the composite solid.

Summary
How did the lessons in this chapter help you find the surface area and volume of a composite solid? *See students' work.*

Lesson 1 Translations

English Learner Instructional Strategy

Language Structure Support: Affixes

Write *transformation, translation, image,* and *congruent* and their Spanish cognates, *transformación, traslación, imagen,* and *congruente,* on the Word Wall. Briefly introduce the meaning of each word, and then, during the lesson, frequently refer to the Word Wall to reinforce meaning and provide concrete examples for each term.

Write *preimage,* underline the prefix *pre-,* and say, *This word part means "before." The preimage is the image **before** it is transformed.* Write *pre-* in a word web, and have students suggest other words they know with the prefix, such as *preview, preteen, prepay, preheat.* Then create a two-column chart labeled *Verb* and *Noun.* Write *transform, transformation, translate,* and *translation* in their respective columns. Write the suffix *-tion* and say, *This word part changes a verb to a noun.* Have students brainstorm other examples to add to the chart, such as *act/action, collect/collection, connect/connection,* and so on.

English Language Development Leveled Activities

Entering/Emerging	Developing/Expanding	Bridging
Academic Vocabulary Have students get into small groups and use a glossary and translation tools to review the lesson's math vocabulary. Direct students to write definitions for the terms in their math notebooks and provide visual examples. Allow students to write the definitions in their own words and/or in their native languages. For *transformation,* be sure students include examples of *slide, flip,* and *turn.* Afterward, regroup students and have them share what they wrote in their journals with the students in another group.	**Anchor Charts** Divide students into four groups. Say, *Make an anchor chart showing different kinds of transformations.* Each chart should include a title at the top of the poster and several labeled examples of different transformations. When the charts are completed, have groups display and describe their charts. Each group's description should use each lesson vocabulary word at least once. List the words for students' reference: *transformation, translation, congruent, image, preimage.*	**Partners Work** Have students work in pairs. Have each pair draw a triangle on a coordinate plane, making sure each point lands where two lines intersect. Then have pairs trade papers. Say, *Translate the figure on the plane. Be sure the new image is congruent to the preimage.* Afterward, have students describe the change in coordinates after the translation. Display the following sentence frames: **The coordinates of the preimage were _____. After we translated the figure, the coordinates became _____.**

Teacher Notes:

NAME _____ DATE _____ PERIOD _____

Lesson 1 Vocabulary
Translations

Use the three-column chart to organize the vocabulary in this lesson. Write the word in Spanish. Then write the definition of each word. Sample answers are given.

English	Spanish	Definition
transformation	transformación	an operation that maps a geometric figure, the preimage, onto a new figure, the image
preimage	preimagen	the original figure before a transformation
image	imagen	the resulting figure after a transformation
translation	traslación	a transformation that slides a figure from one position to another without turning
congruent	congruente	if one image can be obtained by another by a sequence of rotation, reflection, or translations

Module 13 *Transformations, Congruence, and Similarity*   **79**

Lesson 2 Reflections

English Learner Instructional Strategy

Language Structure Support: Modeled Talk

Write *reflection* and *line of reflection* and their Spanish cognates, *reflexión* and *linea de reflexión,* on the Word Wall. Display a mirror and use it to discuss the non-math meaning of *reflection.* Then place the mirror along one of the axes of a coordinate plane. Draw a figure on the plane, and point out how the figure appears to be "reflected" to the opposite side of the axis.

During the lesson, be sure to model clear and correct English pronunciation for students. Whenever possible, have students chorally repeat key words and phrases after you have modeled saying them. Display the following sentence frames to help students during the lesson: **The coordinates are _____. _____ is the line of reflection. The reflection is over the _____.** Be sure students are using subject-verb agreement in differentiating between *is* and *are.* Correct usage as necessary by modeling and then having the student echo.

English Language Development Leveled Activities

Entering/Emerging	Developing/Expanding	Bridging
Choral Responses	**Building Oral Language**	**Academic Word Knowledge**
Give each student an index card. Direct students to write *x-axis* on one side of the card and *y-axis* on the other. As you model reflecting figures across different axes, ask, *Which axis is the line of reflection?* Have students answer by showing you the corresponding side of the index card. Say the answer aloud, *The _____ is the line of reflection,* and have students chorally repeat. After completing multiple examples, draw a figure on the coordinate plane and have a volunteer come forward to complete a reflection per your instruction.	Divide students into groups of four and give each group a blank coordinate plane. Then have the students take turns performing the following tasks: 1) *Draw a three- or four-sided figure within a single quadrant.* 2) *Write the coordinates of the figure.* 3) *Choose an axis as the line of reflection.* 4) *Determine the reflected image's coordinates.* 5) *Use the new coordinates to draw the reflected image and determine correctness.* After groups have completed the tasks, have each student use math vocabulary to describe the step they completed.	Have students work in pairs to write rules for how coordinates change depending over which axis a figure is reflected. Display the following sentence frame for students to use: **When a figure is reflected over the _____, the _____ coordinate stays the same.** Have students share the rules they wrote, and then say, *Write the rules in your math notebook so you can refer to them in the future.*

Teacher Notes:

NAME _____ DATE _____ PERIOD _____

Lesson 2 Vocabulary
Reflections

Use the word cards to define each vocabulary word or phrase and give an example. Sample answers are given.

Word Cards

reflection	reflexión

Definition

a transformation where a

figure is flipped over a line

_____

Definición

transformación en la cual una

figura se voltea sobre una

recta

Example Sentence

A reflection creates a mirror image of the original figure.

When you look in the mirror, you see your reflection.

Word Cards

line of reflection	línea de reflexión

Definition

the line over which a figure is

reflected

_____

Definición

línea a través de la cual se

refleja una figura

Example Sentence

In a reflection, each point of the preimage and its image, are

the same distance from the line of reflection.

80 **Module 13** *Transformations, Congruence, and Similarity*

Lesson 3 Rotations

English Learner Instructional Strategy

Collaborative Support: Numbered Heads Together

Write *rotation* and *rotational symmetry* and their Spanish cognates, *rotación* and *simetría rotacional*, on the Word Wall. Provide meanings and concrete examples for the vocabulary.

Organize students into groups of four and number students as 1–4. Assign one problem to each group. They should discuss the problem, agree on a solution, and ensure that everyone in the group understands and can give the answer. Afterward, call out a random number from 1 to 4. Have students assigned to that number raise their hands, and when called on, answer for their team.

Display the following sentence frames for students who need additional help:
I don't understand _____. What does _____ mean? I need help with _____.

English Language Development Leveled Activities

Entering/Emerging	Developing/Expanding	Bridging
Number Game	**Report Back**	**Pass the Pen**
Write: *1) clockwise* and *2) counterclockwise*. Divide students into two teams. Place an object with rotational symmetry onto a table, and have a student from one of the teams come forward. Have the students of the other team choose a direction (clockwise or counterclockwise) and chorally say either **1** or **2**, or say **clockwise/ counterclockwise**. The student scores a point for his or her team by turning the object in the correct direction. Have teams take turns giving directions and following directions. Continue until one team has 5 points.	Create a set of cards describing rotations, such as *90° clockwise about a point; 180° counterclockwise about the origin;* and so on. Have students pair up, and then randomly distribute one card to each pair. Direct students to draw a figure on a coordinate plane and then rotate the figure according to what is shown on the card they received. Have pairs exchange graphs (but not cards) and then describe the rotation on the coordinate plane they were given using the following sentence frame: **The figure has been rotated _____ degrees about [a/the] _____.**	Divide students into four groups and assign a problem to each group. Have students work jointly on the problem by passing a copy of the problem around the table to complete each step. Direct each member of the group to write a sentence or phrase on a strip of paper describing the step he or she has completed. Afterward, have groups share their work, and have each student read the sentence they wrote.

Teacher Notes:

NAME _____ DATE _____ PERIOD _____

Lesson 3 Vocabulary
Rotations

Use the concept web to name the transformation and the parts of the
transformation. Sample answers are given.

Word Bank	
center of rotation	image
preimage	rotation

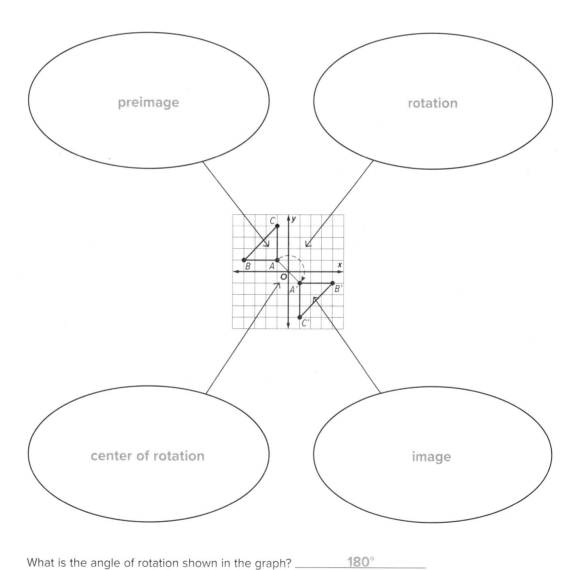

What is the angle of rotation shown in the graph? _____180°_____

Lesson 4 Dilations

English Learner Instructional Strategy

Vocabulary Support: Build Background Knowledge

To support students' vocabulary acquisition on a regular basis, encourage them to scan their texts to identify words that are unfamiliar. Have students read the words aloud or, if they are unsure of pronunciation, by spelling the words. Create a list of the words, and then review each by having students refer to a glossary, their math notebook, the Word Wall, the classroom anchor charts, or other reference sources.

If Entering/Emerging students have difficulty with non-math vocabulary during the lesson, encourage them to ask more proficient English-speaking peers for help. Display sentence frames to help students ask for clarification for unfamiliar vocabulary: **What is _____? I don't understand the word _____. How do I say this word?**

English Language Development Leveled Activities

Entering/Emerging	Developing/Expanding	Bridging
Academic Vocabulary	**Act It Out**	**Anchor Charts**
Write *enlargement* and underline *large*. Say, *If I make something larger, I make an enlargement.* Say *enlargement* again, slowly and clearly, and have student chorally repeat. Then write *reduction* and underline *reduc*. Say, *If I make something smaller, I reduce its size. I make a reduction.* Say *reduction* again and have students repeat chorally. Then display examples of reductions and enlargements on coordinate planes. Have students identify them by chorally saying **reduction** or **enlargement** or by pointing to the correct word.	Have students work in pairs. Distribute copies of a map showing North and South America to each pair. Say, *Choose a state or country where you have lived, visited, or would like to go visit.* Have pairs lay tracing paper on the map and use a ruler to draw a rectangle around the chosen state or country. Then direct students to determine the scale factor they would use to enlarge the rectangle to fill most of an $8\frac{1}{2} \times 11$ sheet of paper. Afterward, have pairs share the place they chose and why, and identify the scale factor of enlargement.	Have students work in pairs to create anchor charts for the vocabulary word *dilation*. Give each pair a number cube. Say, *Roll your number cube. If you roll 1, roll again. The number you roll is the scale factor you will use for the enlargement shown on your chart.* Direct pairs to write *Dilations* at the top of the chart and include definitions and labeled examples for *dilation, enlargement, reduction,* and *scale factor.* Ask each pair to show the other students their chart and justify their examples.

Teacher Notes:

NAME _____ DATE _____ PERIOD _____

Lesson 4 Review Vocabulary

Dilations

Use the definition map to list qualities about the vocabulary word or phrase.
Sample answers are given.

Vocabulary

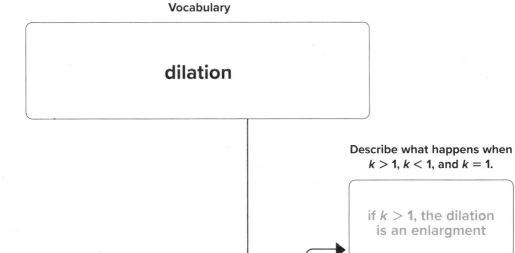

dilation

Describe what happens when
$k > 1$, $k < 1$, and $k = 1$.

if $k > 1$, the dilation
is an enlargment

Description

a transformation that
enlarges or reduces a figure
by a scale factor of k

if $k < 1$, the dilation
is a reduction

if $k = 1$, the dilation
will be the same size
as the original figure

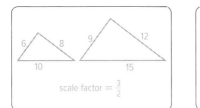

scale factor = $\frac{3}{2}$

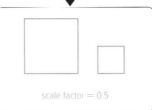

scale factor = 0.5

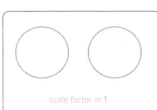

scale factor = 1

Draw and label examples for $k > 1$, $k < 1$, and $k = 1$.

Lesson 5 Congruence and Transformations

English Learner Instructional Strategy

Sensory Support: Magazines and Newspapers

Divide students into small groups consisting of students with differing levels of English proficiency. Provide each group with a selection of magazines or newspapers. Direct students to search for examples of figures that have been rotated, reflected, or translated to create a logo or other graphic design. Say, *Try to find at least one example each of a reflection, rotation, and translation.* Display the following tiered sentence frames for students to describe the examples:

Entering/Emerging: **It is a [reflection/rotation/translation].**
Developing/Expanding: **This _____ has been [reflected/rotated/translated].**
Bridging: **This is an example of a [reflection/rotation/translation] because _____.**

English Language Development Leveled Activities

Entering/Emerging	Developing/Expanding	Bridging
Developing Oral Language	**Word Recognition**	**Pass the Pen**
Help students with the /ed/ sound used to indicate past tense. Write *rotated, reflected,* and *translated.* Distribute a variety of two-dimensional figure manipulatives to students, and then have them take turns tracing the figures according to your directive: [*Reflect/Rotate/Translate*] *the figure.* After each student's turn, have the student describe what he or she did using a word from the board: **I _____ the figure.** Listen for the /ed/ sound. If needed, remodel and have the student echo.	Create a large set of cards describing transformations. (e.g., *rotate 90° clockwise; reflect vertically; translate to the left; rotate 45° counterclockwise;* and so on.) Distribute a variety of two-dimensional figure manipulatives to students. Have each student randomly select two cards. Say, *Transform your figure in the two ways shown on your cards.* Students complete the task tracing the preimage and the final transformed image. Have students take turns describing what they did: **First, I _____. Then, I _____.**	Divide students into four groups and assign a problem to each group. Have students pass a copy of the problem around the table to complete each step. Direct each member of the group to write a sentence or phrase on a strip of paper describing the step he or she completed. Afterward, have groups share their completed work, and have each student read the sentence they wrote.

Multicultural Teacher Tip

At times, communication with ELLs may prove difficult. Be patient and focus as much as possible on what the student means versus how he or she is saying it. If students are more comfortable with written versus verbal English, encourage them to write out solutions or steps leading to an answer. Allow students to use their native language if attempts at English are hindering their abilities to reason out the solution to a problem.

NAME _____ DATE _____ PERIOD _____

Lesson 5 Review Vocabulary

Congruence and Transformations

Use the definition map to list qualities about the vocabulary word or phrase.
Sample answers are given.

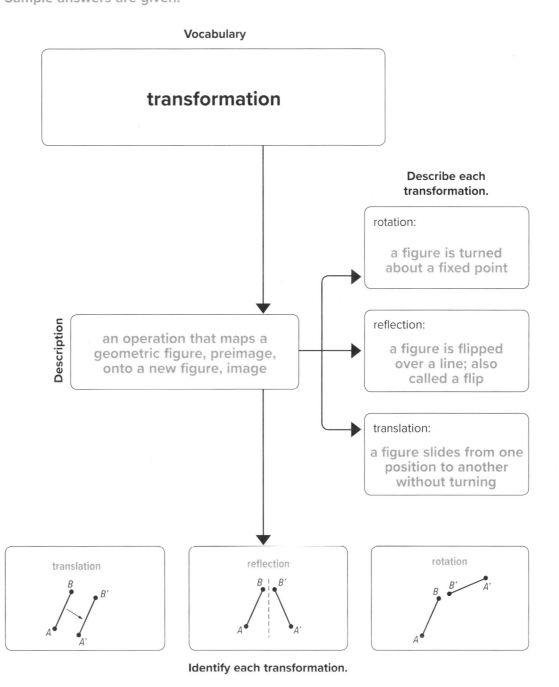

Vocabulary

transformation

Describe each
transformation.

rotation:

a figure is turned
about a fixed point

reflection:

a figure is flipped
over a line; also
called a flip

translation:

a figure slides from one
position to another
without turning

Description

an operation that maps a
geometric figure, preimage,
onto a new figure, image

translation

reflection

rotation

Identify each transformation.

Lesson 6 Similarity and Transformations

English Learner Instructional Strategy

Graphic Support: Graphic Organizers

Write *similar* and *scale factor* and their Spanish cognate, *similar* and *factor de escala,* on the Word Wall. To provide a concrete example for *similar,* compare two similar but not identical objects, such as a pair of pencils or different-colored connecting cubes. Then create a two-column chart labeled *Similar* and *Same,* and have students brainstorm examples that could go in each column. You might also include the English and Spanish spellings of *similar* in the *Same* column and the spellings of *scale* and *escala* in the *Similar* column.

For *scale factor,* have students look up the everyday meanings of each word. Use a Venn diagram to compare and discuss the everyday meanings with the math meanings. In the middle section of the diagram, record how the meanings are related.

English Language Development Leveled Activities

Entering/Emerging	Developing/Expanding	Bridging
Number Sense	**Show What You Know**	**Listen and Write**
Create a set of scale factor cards. Be sure to include values less than one, equal to one, and greater than one. Write *bigger, same, smaller.* As each student takes a turn drawing a card, say, *The scale factor is _____. Will the new figure be* **bigger, the same,** *or* **smaller?** Have the student answer, either by saying the word or by pointing to the correct word. If the student answers with a gesture, say the word and encourage him or her to echo. Continue until all students have had a turn.	Distribute a coordinate grid to pairs of students. Direct pairs to draw a triangle or quadrilateral in one of the quadrants. Then have them use a virtual three section (red, blue, and yellow) spinner to determine a scale factor for dilating their figure. Use the following values: $red = \frac{1}{2}$, *blue = 2, yellow = 3.* Have students draw the new figure, dilated by the determined scale factor and transformed one other way. Then have students describe the transformations using sentence frames: **The scale factor was _____. We also _____ the figure. The two figures are _____. (similar)**	Divide students into small groups. Say, *Listen and take notes. Then work together to answer the questions.* Read aloud the following problem: An art show offers different sizes of the same painting. The original print is 24 cm by 30 cm. A printer enlarges the original by a scale factor of 1.5 and then enlarges the second image by a scale factor of 3. What are the dimensions of the largest print? Are both of the enlarged prints similar to the original? Read slowly and enunciate clearly. Give groups time to complete the first question before asking the second one. Display sentence frames to help students share their answers: **The largest print is _____ centimeters by _____ centimeters. The enlarged prints are _____ because _____.**

Teacher Notes:

NAME _____ DATE _____ PERIOD _____

Lesson 6 Vocabulary
Similarity and Transformations

Use the definition map to list qualities about the vocabulary word or phrase.
Sample answers are given.

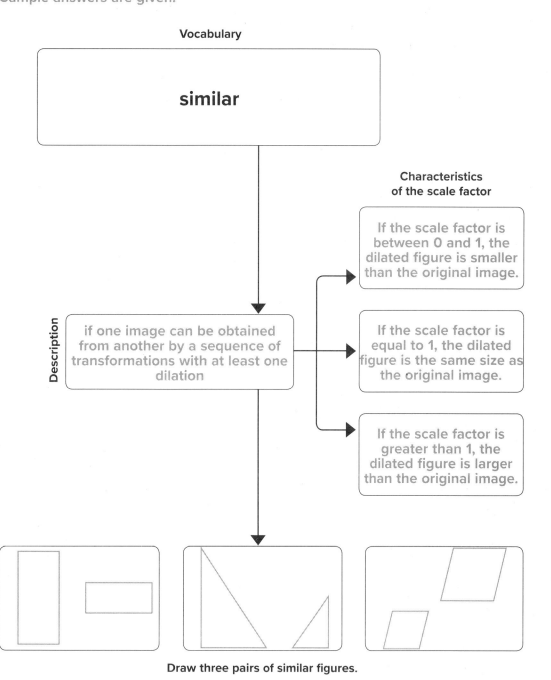

Vocabulary

similar

**Characteristics
of the scale factor**

If the scale factor is
between 0 and 1, the
dilated figure is smaller
than the original image.

Description

if one image can be obtained
from another by a sequence of
transformations with at least one
dilation

If the scale factor is
equal to 1, the dilated
figure is the same size as
the original image.

If the scale factor is
greater than 1, the
dilated figure is larger
than the original image.

Draw three pairs of similar figures.

Lesson 7 Indirect Measurement

English Learner Instructional Strategy

Sensory Support: Pictures and Photographs

Write *direct* and *indirect*. Underline the prefix *in-*, and say, *This word part means "not," so* ***indirect*** *means "not direct."* Have students brainstorm other examples of words that use the prefix *in-*, such as *incomplete, incorrect, informal, insecure, inaccurate.* Be sure to point out that not all words that start with *in-* use this meaning.

Create a two-column chart labeled *Direct* and *Indirect*. Show students photographs or illustrations of objects in a wide variety of sizes. For each object, ask students whether it would be measured directly or indirectly. Have students answer by saying **direct** or **indirect.** Tape up the photo or illustration in the corresponding column of the chart. Be sure students are saying the /ct/ sound at the end of each word. Some languages, including Spanish, do not commonly use consonant blends as final sounds, so the pronunciation may give students trouble. Model pronunciation as needed and have students chorally repeat.

English Language Development Leveled Activities

Entering/Emerging	Developing/Expanding	Bridging
Choral Responses	**Numbered Heads Together**	**Show What You Know**
Write *add* (+), *subtract* (−), *multiply* (×), *divide* (÷). As you work through examples, refer to the operations as you use them to solve the indirect measurement problems. As you say each term, have students chorally respond by repeating the word back to you. Continue in this manner as you model solving the following problem: *At the same time a 2-meter street sign casts a 3-meter shadow, a nearby telephone pole casts a 12.3-meter shadow. How tall is the telephone pole?* In addition, invite a volunteer to draw diagrams showing the sign, the pole, and their shadows. Direct the student to outline the similar triangles, and then use the ratios of corresponding sides to solve.	Organize students into groups of four and number off the students in each group as 1–4. Assign a problem to each group. Have the students in each group discuss the problem, agree on a solution, and ensure that everyone in the group understands and can give the answer. Afterward, call out a random number from 1 to 4. Have students assigned to that number raise their hands, and when called on, answer for their team.	Divide students into three groups, and give each group a sheet of drawing paper. Say, *Create your own indirect measurement problem. Use problems from the lesson as a guide.* After groups have completed the task, have them exchange papers and solve the problem they were given. Then have volunteers from each group describe the problem and how they solved for the unknown measurement.

Teacher Notes:

Lesson 7 Vocabulary

Indirect Measurement

Use the flow chart to solve a problem using indirect measurement.
Sample answers are given.

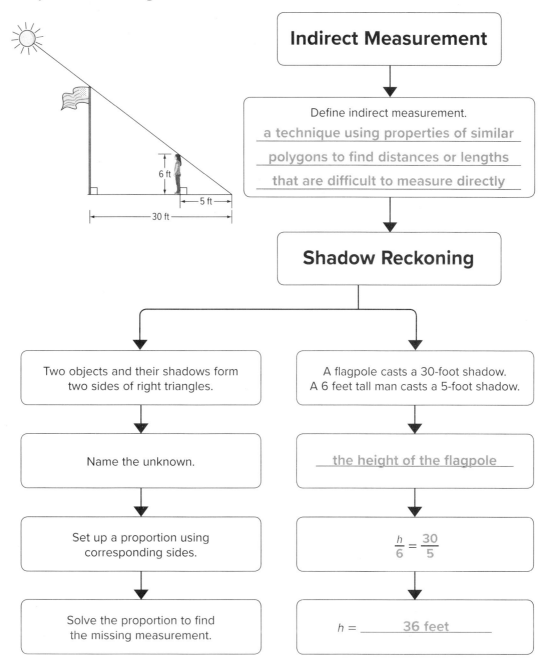

Indirect Measurement

Define indirect measurement.
<u>a technique using properties of similar</u>
<u>polygons to find distances or lengths</u>
<u>that are difficult to measure directly</u>

Shadow Reckoning

Two objects and their shadows form two sides of right triangles.

A flagpole casts a 30-foot shadow. A 6 feet tall man casts a 5-foot shadow.

Name the unknown.

<u>the height of the flagpole</u>

Set up a proportion using corresponding sides.

$\frac{h}{6} = \frac{30}{5}$

Solve the proportion to find the missing measurement.

$h = $ <u>36 feet</u>

Module 13 *Transformations, Congruence, and Similarity* **85**

What are VKVs and who needs them?

"VKVs are flashcards that animate words by kinesthetically focusing on their structure, use, and meaning. VKVs are beneficial not only to students learning the specialized vocabulary of a content area, but also to students learning the vocabulary of a second language."

Dinah Zike | Educational Consultant

Dinah-Might Activities, Inc. – San Antonio, Texas

Why did you invent VKVs?

"Twenty years ago, I began designing flashcards that would accomplish the same thing with academic vocabulary and cognates that Foldables® do with general information, concepts, and ideas—make them a visual, kinesthetic, and memorable experience."

Dinah Zike's
Visual Kinesthetic Vocabulary

I had three goals in mind:

- **Making two-dimensional flashcards three-dimensional**

- **Designing flashcards that allow one or more parts of a word or phrase to be manipulated and changed to form numerous terms based upon a commonality**

- **Using one sheet or strip of paper to make purposefully shaped flashcards that were neither glued nor stapled, but could be folded to the same height, making them easy to stack and store**

Why are VKVs important in today's classroom?

"At the beginning of this century, research and reports indicated the importance of vocabulary to overall academic achievement. This research resulted in a more comprehensive teaching of academic vocabulary and a focus on the use of cognates to help students learn a second language. Teachers know the importance of using a variety of strategies to teach vocabulary to a diverse population of students. VKVs function as one of those strategies."

An Interview with
Dinah Zike Explaining
Visual Kinesthetic Vocabulary®, or VKVs®

Dinah Zike's
Visual
Kinesthetic
Vocabulary

How are VKVs used to teach content vocabulary to EL students?

" VKVs can be used to show the similarities between cognates in Spanish and English. For example, by folding and unfolding specially designed VKVs, students can experience English terms in one color and Spanish in a second color on the same flashcard while noting the similarities in their roots. "

What organization and usage hints would you give teachers using VKVs?

" Cut off the flap of a 6" x 9" envelope and slightly widen the envelope's opening by cutting away a shallow V or half circle on one side only. Glue the non-cut side of the envelope into the front or back of student notebooks or journals. VKVs can be stored in this pocket.

Encourage students to individualize their flashcards by writing notes, sketching diagrams, recording examples, forming plurals (radius: radii or radiuses), and noting when the math terms presented are homophones (sine/sign) or contain root words or combining forms (kilo-, milli-, tri-).

As students make and use the flashcards included in this text, they will learn how to design their own VKVs. Provide time for students to design, create, and share their flashcards with classmates. "

Dinah Zike's book Foldables, Notebook Foldables, & VKVs for Spelling and Vocabulary 4th-12th won a Teachers' Choice Award in 2011 for "instructional value, ease of use, quality, and innovation"; it has become a popular methods resource for teaching and learning vocabulary.

Dinah Zike's
Visual
Kinesthetic
Vocabulary

 cut on all dashed lines

 fold on all solid lines

Solve the proportion. (Resuelve una proporción.)

$$\frac{6}{x} = \frac{5}{8}$$

proportion

proporción

In math, a proportion is an equation stating that (en matemáticas, una proporción es una ecuación que indica que).

direct

variación

Does the graph show a direct variation? Explain. (¿El gráfico muestra una variación directa? Explique.)

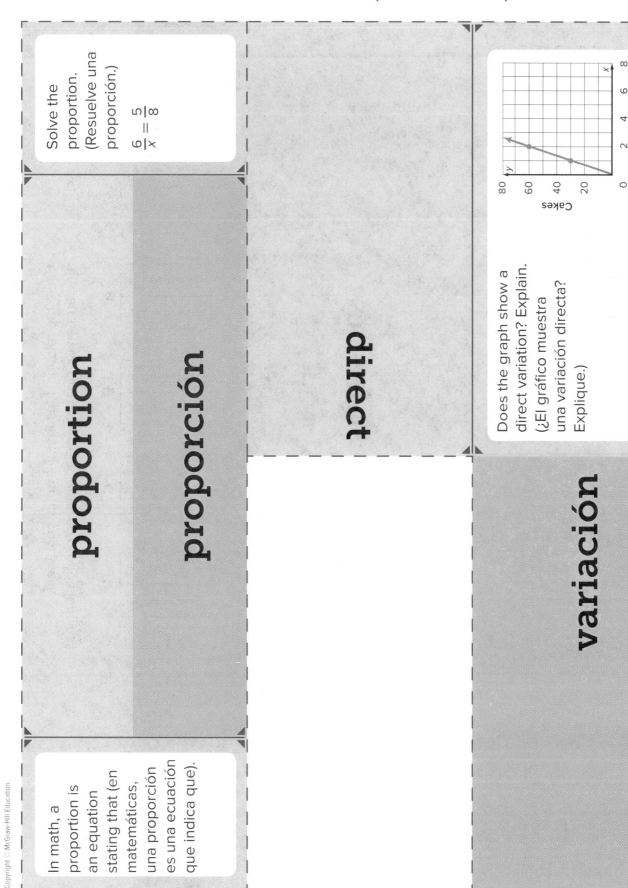

Dinah Zike's
Visual
Kinesthetic
Vocabulary

VKV

✂ cut on all dashed lines   ⬜ fold on all solid lines

al

al

al

directa

variation

no

non

The equation $y = 70x$ shows how many cars y cross a bridge in x hours. On a separate sheet of paper, graph the equation. Is it a direct variation? If so, what is the constant of proportionality? (La ecuación $y = 70x$ expresa cuántos carros y cruzan un puente en x horas. Has una gráfica de la ecuación en orta hoja. ¿Es una ecuación de variación directa? Si es así, ¿cuál es la constante de proporcionalidad?)

Circle the relationships that are nonproportional. (Encierra en un círculo las relaciones no proporcionales.)

A
x	y
2	4
5	7
7	9

B
x	y
1	6
3	18
5	30

C
x	y
0	3
1	6
2	9

D
x	y
2	4
5	10
8	16

Dinah Zike's
Visual Kinesthetic Vocabulary

✂ cut on all dashed lines

▭ fold on all solid lines

Define percent error.
(Define porcentaje de error.)

_____

_____

_____

percent error

Write each number as a percent. (Escribar cada número como un porcentaje.)

0.25 = _____ %

$\frac{5}{6}$ = _____ %

12 = _____ %

$\frac{9}{10}$ = _____ %

de error

porcentaje

Sofia estimated that a drive to the beach would take 3 hours. The actual drive lasted for 3 hours and 25 minutes. What was the percent error of Sofia's estimate? (Sofía cálculo que un recorrido en auto hasta la playa tardaría 3 horas. El recorrido real tardó 3 horas y 25 minutos. ¿Cual fue el porcentaje de error en el cálculo de Sofia?)

Answer: about _____ %

Dinah Zike's
Visual
Kinesthetic
Vocabulary

✂ cut on all dashed lines

⬒ fold on all solid lines

Write the additive inverse of each number below. (Escribe el inverso aditivo de los siguientes números.)

13 _____ −2 _____

−25 _____ 1 _____

additive inverse

Define additive inverse. (Define inverso aditivo.)

Define absolute value. (Define valor absoluto.)

absolute value

aditivo

inverso

Circle the word that has the same meaning as *additive inverse*. (Encierra en un círculo la palabra que significa lo mismo que inverso aditivo.)

negative integer   opposite

number line   absolute value

valor absoluto

Evaluate each expression. (Evalúa cada expresión.)

|−23| = _____ |8| = _____

|−7| + |10| = _____ |−16| − |9| = _____

Dinah Zike's
Visual Kinesthetic Vocabulary

✂ cut on all dashed lines

✁ fold on all solid lines

rational number

Define rational number. (Define número racional.)

número racional

List three different forms of rational numbers. (Enumera tres formas de representar los números racionales.)

Write the opposite of each number below.
(Escribe el opuesto de los siguientes números.)

12 _____

−54 _____

−16 _____

25 _____

Explain how to graph an integer on a number line. (Explica cómo representar gráficamente un entero en una recta numérica.)

opposites

graph

Dinah Zike's
Visual
Kinesthetic
Vocabulary

✂ cut on all dashed lines

⬜ fold on all solid lines

ficar

uestos

Graph –6, 2, 8, and –3 on the number line. (Representa gráficamente –6, 2, 8, y –3 en la recta numérica.)

-8 -6 -4 -2 0 2 4 6 8 10 12

Explain why 6 and –6 are opposites. (Explica por qué 6 y –6 son opuestos.)

VKV12 **Visual Kinesthetic Learning**

Why is bar notation used to represent repeating decimals? (¿Por qué la notación de barras se utiliza para representar números decimales periódicos?)

bar notation

What does the bar in 0.1$\overline{6}$ mean? (¿Qué significa la barra sobre 0.1$\overline{6}$?)

How does writing fractions with a common denominator help you compare them? (¿De qué forma escribir fracciones con un común denominador te ayuda a compararlas entre sí?)

common denominator

Dinah Zike's
Visual
Kinesthetic
Vocabulary

 cut on all dashed lines

 fold on all solid lines

de barra

común denominador

Use bar notation to rewrite each decimal. (Vuelve a escribir cada número decimal con notación de barras.)

0.7777 . . . = _____

9.3555 . . . = _____

−0.337337 . . . = _____

Rewrite $\frac{1}{8}$ and $\frac{1}{5}$ with a common denominator.

(Escribe $\frac{1}{8}$ y $\frac{1}{5}$ de manera que ambos tengan un común denominador.)

$$\frac{1}{5} = \underline{\hspace{2cm}}$$

$$\frac{1}{8} = \underline{\hspace{2cm}}$$

notación

VKV14   Visual Kinesthetic Learning

 cut on all dashed lines

 fold on all solid lines

Define exponent. (Define exponente.)

_____

_____

_____

Circle the irrational number.

Spanish Translation

$\frac{5}{8}$ −6.5   12%

$\sqrt{8}$ 0.2222 . . .

exponente

b^x

base

racional

irrational number

Define base. (Define base.)

_____

_____

_____

Dinah Zike's
Visual
Kinesthetic
Vocabulary

✄ cut on all dashed lines

✂ fold on all solid lines

exponent

x

Rewrite as a power. (Reescribe como potencia.)

$6 \times 6 \times 6 \times 6 \times 6 =$ _____

The base is (La base es) _____

The exponent is (El exponente es) _____.

base

b

número   irracionales

rational

A rational number can be expressed as (un número racional se puede expresar como)

_____

✂ cut on all dashed lines   ⬜ fold on all solid lines

Write about a time when you would use scientific notation. (Escribe sobre una situación en la cual usarías la notación científica.)

Circle the perfect cubes. (Encierra en un círculo los cubos perfectos.)

6   9   27

125   200   625

Circle the radical sign. (Encierra en un círculo el signo radical.)

$\sqrt{}$ +

$\times$

scientific notation

perfect cube

radical sign

Circle the numbers written in scientific notation. (Encierra en un círculo los números escritos en notación científica.)

0.034 2.75×10^5

3×10^{-4} 98.3

Find each cube root. (Halla la raíz cúbica.)

$\sqrt[3]{-27} =$ _____

$\sqrt[3]{216} =$ _____

$\sqrt[3]{8,000} =$ _____

Simplify the expression. (Simplifica la expresión.)

$\sqrt[3]{216} =$ _____

Dinah Zike's
Visual
Kinesthetic
Vocabulary

 cut on all dashed lines

 fold on all solid lines

radical

perfecto

científica

A radical sign is used to (El signo radical se usa para)

1,728 is a perfect cube. Explain why. (1,728 es cubo perfecto. Explica por qué.)

Write 263,000 in scientific notation. (Escribe 263,000 en notación científica.)

Write 8.64×10^4 in standard form. (Escribe 8.64×10^4 en forma estándar.)

signo

cubo

notación

Define coefficient. (Define coeficiente.)

coefficient

Rewrite $9x - 15y$ in factored form. (Escribe la forma factorizada de la función $9x - 15y$.)

factored form

What property is used when factoring a linear expression? (¿Qué propiedad se utiliza para factorizar una función lineal?)

Circle the greatest common factor of $15x$ and $27xy$. (Encierra en un círculo el máximo común divisor de $15x$ y $27xy$.)

3	3x	y
5	x	9

factor

✂ cut on all dashed lines

▱ fold on all solid lines

izar

factorizada

iciente

Write about a time when writing a linear expression in factored form might be useful. (Escribe sobre una situación en la que sería útil escribir la forma factorizada de una función lineal.)

Circle the coefficient in each expression. (Encierra en un círculo el coeficiente de cada expresión.)

$12 - 5x$ $19m - 24$

$9p + 17r$ $37 + 11a$

Factor each expression. (Factoriza cada expresión.)

$12x + 3 = $ _____

$27a + 12b = $ _____

$16m - 18 = $ _____

forma

Find the GCF of the pair of monomials. (Halla el MCD de ambos monomios.)

6x, 21xy

_____

expression

monomial

lineal

Is $a^2 - 6$ a linear expression? Explain. (¿Es la expresión $a^2 - 6$ una función lineal? Explica.)

✂ cut on all dashed lines

▱ fold on all solid lines

expresión

linear

Write two examples of linear expressions. (Escribe dos ejemplos de funciones lineales.)

Define monomial. (Define monomio.)

✂ cut on all dashed lines

📦 fold on all solid lines

What value of x makes the equation true? (¿Qué valor de x hace la ecuación verdadera?)

$x + 8 = 13$ _____

solution

Circle the equations that are equivalent to $x = 9$. (Encierra en un círculo las ecuaciones equivalentes a $x = 9$.)

$x + 12 = 20$ $x - 5 = 4$ $3 + x = 12$

equivalent equation

ción

ecuación equivalente

Find the solution of each equation. (Halla la solución de cada ecuación.)

$x - 12 = 8$

_____

$9 + y = 17$

_____

Are the equations $x + 11 = 14$ and $x = 3$ equivalent? Explain. (¿Son las ecuaciones $x + 11 = 14$ and $x = 3$ equivalentes? Explica.)

_____
_____
_____
_____

✂ cut on all dashed lines

📄 fold on all solid lines

Circle the multiplicative inverse of $\frac{5}{9}$. (Encierra en un círculo el inverso multiplicativo de $\frac{5}{9}$.)

$\frac{10}{18}$

$\frac{9}{5}$

$\frac{5}{9}$

$\frac{18}{10}$

Circle the identity. (Encierra en un círculo la identidad.)

$\frac{3}{4} - 12y = y + 1$

$12p + 6 = 6 + 12p$

$12x = 60$

$9s = 24 + s$

multiplicative inverse

identity

Solve the equation using the multiplicative inverse. (Utiliza el inverso multiplicativo para resolver la ecuación.)

$\frac{3}{4}x = 2\frac{5}{8}$

multiplicativo

dad

The product of a number and its multiplicative inverse is (El producto de un número y su inverso multiplicativo es)

_____ .

An identity is an equation that is (Una identidad es una ecuación que es)

_____ .

What is the opposite of an identity? (¿Que es lo contrario de una identidad?)

_____ .

inverso

Define linear relationship.
(Define relación lineal.)

linear relationship

What does a linear relationship look like when it is graphed? (¿Cómo se ve la gráfica de una relación lineal?)

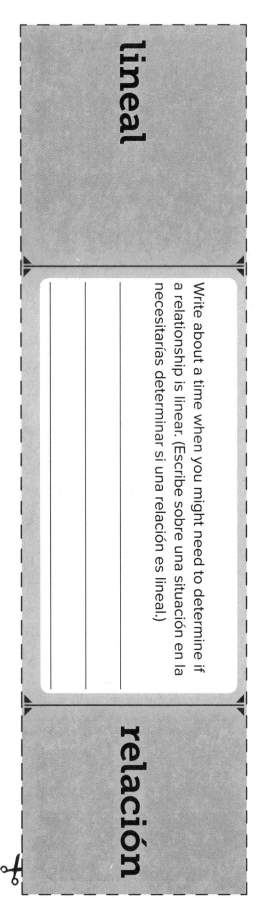

lineal

Write about a time when you might need to determine if a relationship is linear. (Escribe sobre una situación en la necesitarías determinar si una relación es lineal.)

relación

✂ cut on all dashed lines

▭ fold on all solid lines

Define simulation. (Define simulación.)

simulation

Dinah Zike's
Visual
Kinesthetic
Vocabulary

✂ cut on all dashed lines

⬒ fold on all solid lines

ción

Describe a model to represent choosing one pair of socks at random from a drawer with six pairs total. (Describe un modelo que represente la elección al azar de un par de calcetines en un cajón de seis pares de calcetines.)

Dinah Zike's
VKV

✂ cut on all dashed lines

fold on all solid lines

theoretical probability

experimental

What is the theoretical probability of rolling a 3 with a number cube? (¿Cuál es la probabilidad teórica de obtener un 3 al lanzar un dado?)

_____

Dinah Zike's
Visual
Kinesthetic
Vocabulary

✂ cut on all dashed lines

fold on all solid lines

probabilidad teórica

experimental

Using a number cube, you roll a 5 four times out of 18 total rolls. What is the experimental probability of rolling another 5? (En dieciocho lanzamientos de un dado, obtienes un 5 cuatro veces. ¿Cuál es la probabilidad experimental de obtener otro 5?)

cut on all dashed lines

fold on all solid lines

Define population. (Define población.)

statistics

population

Dinah Zike's
Visual Kinesthetic Vocabulary
VKV

✂ cut on all dashed lines

▱ fold on all solid lines ◂

dística

ción

e

Statistics deal with _____, and _____ data. (La estadística tiene que ver con _____, _____ y _____, de datos.)

You want to survey customers at a store to see which dog food is most popular. The population is _____. The sample is _____. (Vas a hacer una encuesta a los clientes de un almacén para averiguar cuál comida para perros es más popular. La población es _____. La muestra es _____.)

Dinah Zike's
Visual Kinesthetic Vocabulary

✂ cut on all dashed lines

⬜ fold on all solid lines

factor de

scale model

What is the scale factor of a dollhouse if 5 centimeters represents 1 meter? (¿Cuál es el factor de escala de una casa de muñecas en la que 5 centímetros representan un metro?)

modelo a escala

factor

List three examples where you might find scale models used. (Menciona tres situaciones en las que se utilizan modelos a escala.)

cut on all dashed lines

fold on all solid lines

center

nferencia

circle

Define center. (Define centro.)

Define circle. (Define círculo.)

Copyright © McGraw-Hill Education.

Visual Kinesthetic Learning   VKV37

circumference

írculo

Use *center* to describe the radius and diameter of a circle. (Utiliza la palabra *centro* para describir el radio y el diámetro de un círculo.)

Find the circumference. (Halla la circunferencia.)

15 m

ro

A circle's diameter is _____ the length of the circle's radius. (El diámetro de un círculo es el _____ de la longitud del radio del círculo.)

If you know the length of a circle's radius, what three other measurements can you find? (¿Cuáles tres medidas puedes calcular con la longitud del radio de un círculo?)

Describe a real-world composite figure, explaining the object's purpose, and the figures of which it is composed. (Describe un objeto real cuya forma sea una figura compuesta. Explica su función y menciona las figuras de las cuales se compone.)

diameter

radius

composite figure

Define composite figure. (Define figura compuesto.)

compuesto

o

ámetro

Use two polygons to draw a composite figure. (Dibuja una figura compuesta por dos polígonos.)

figura

Draw a radius of the circle. (Dibuja el radio del círculo.)

Draw a diameter of the circle. (Dibuja el diámetro del círculo.)

✂ cut on all dashed lines

⌂ fold on all solid lines

The formula for the area of a circle is $A = \pi r^2$. Write the formula for the area of a semicircle. (La fórmula para calcular el área de un círculo es $A = \pi r^2$. Escribe la fórmula para calcular el área de un semicírculo.)

$A =$ _____

semicircle

lateral surface area

Define lateral surface area. (Define área de superficie lateral.)

Dinah Zike's
Visual Kinesthetic Vocabulary

✂ cut on all dashed lines

fold on all solid lines

área de superficie lateral

írculo

Find the area of the semicircle. (Calcula el área del semicírculo.)

14 yd

Find the lateral surface area of the figure. Use the formula $L.A. = \frac{1}{2}P\ell$ (Utiliza la fórmula $S.L. = \frac{1}{2}P\ell$ para calcular la superficie lateral de la figura.)

16 m
16 m
20 m
16 m

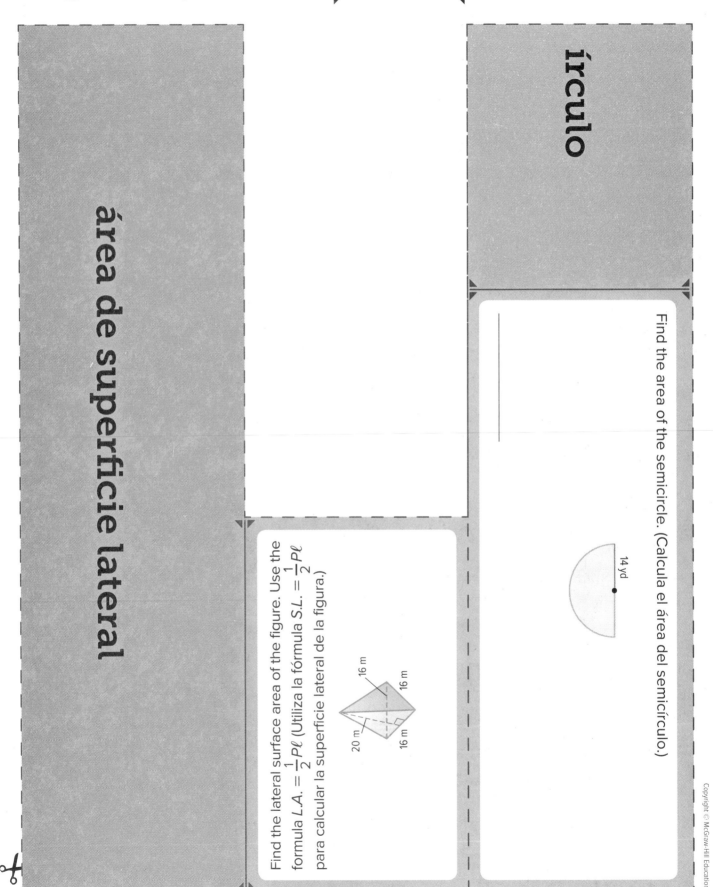

Dinah Zike's
Visual
Kinesthetic
Vocabulary

 cut on all dashed lines

fold on all solid lines

How many planes intersect to form a cube? (¿Cuantos planos se intersecan en un cubo?)

ilindro

Define congruent. (Define congruente.)

Cones and cylinders are not polyhedrons. Explain why. (Explica por qué los conos y los cilindros no son poliedros.)

plane

cone

congruent

Dinah Zike's
VKV
Visual
Kinesthetic
Vocabulary

✂ cut on all dashed lines

⬚ fold on all solid lines

e

o

O

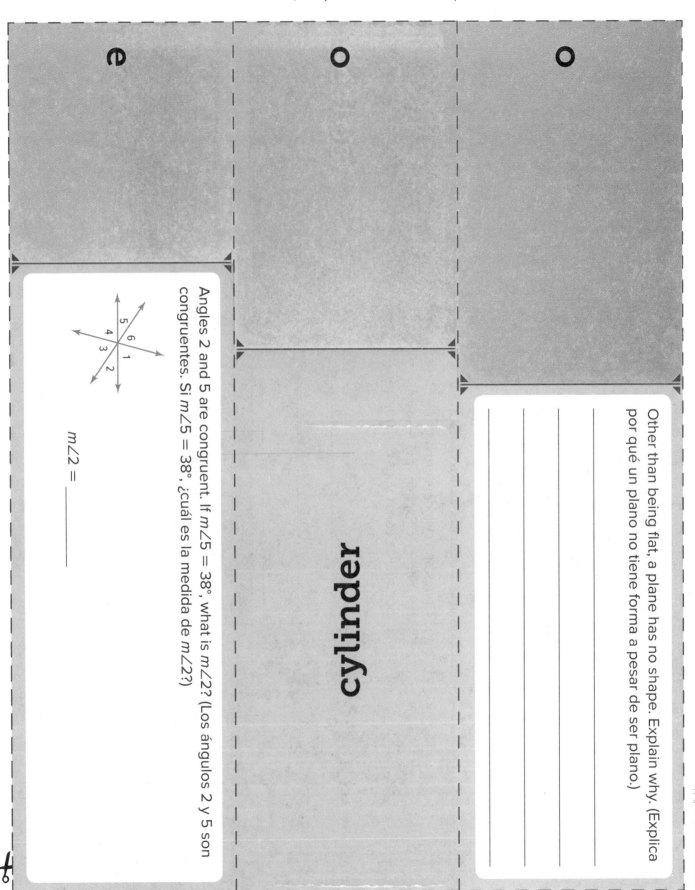

Angles 2 and 5 are congruent. If $m\angle 5 = 38°$, what is $m\angle 2$? (Los ángulos 2 y 5 son congruentes. Si $m\angle 5 = 38°$, ¿cuál es la medida de $m\angle 2$?)

$m\angle 2 =$ _____

cylinder

Other than being flat, a plane has no shape. Explain why. (Explica por qué un plano no tiene forma a pesar de ser plano.)

Dinah Zike's
VKV Visual
Kinesthetic
Vocabulary

✂ cut on all dashed lines

⬜ fold on all solid lines

regular pyramid

The base of a regular pyramid is a regular _____.
(La base de una pirámide regular es un _____.)

Dinah Zike's
**Visual
Kinesthetic
Vocabulary**

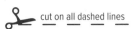 cut on all dashed lines

 fold on all solid lines

pirámide regular

Define regular pyramid. (Define pirámide regular.)

Use the figure below to complete the following equation. (Completa la ecuación con ayuda de la siguiente figura.)

$$m\angle 6 = m\angle \underline{\quad} + m\angle \underline{\quad}$$

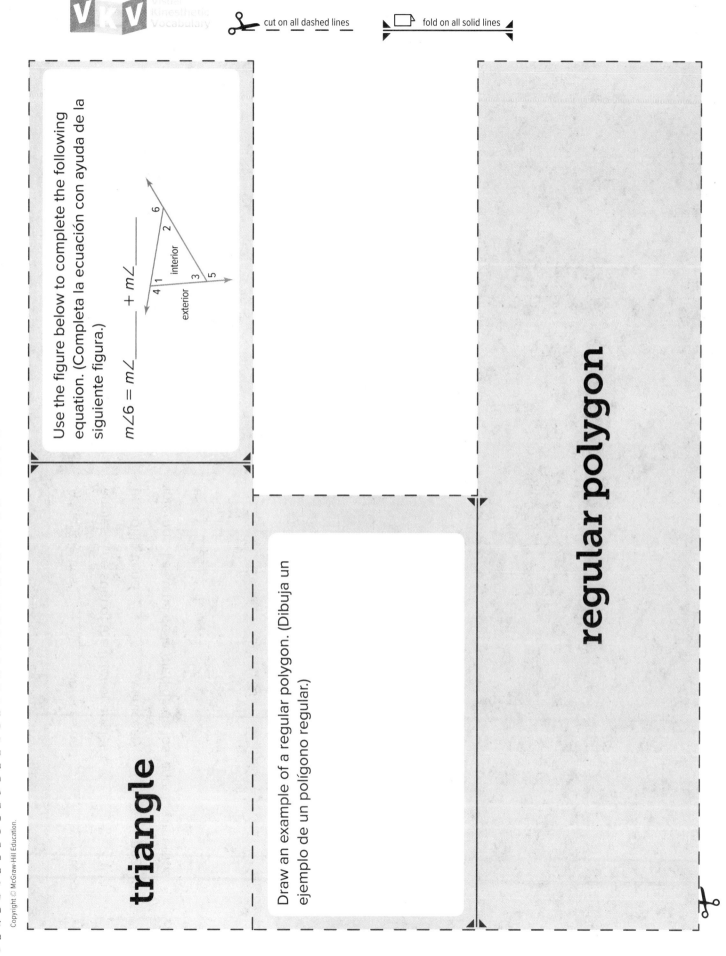

triangle

Draw an example of a regular polygon. (Dibuja un ejemplo de un polígono regular.)

regular polygon

ángulo

polígono regular

A triangle has _____ vertices and _____ interior angles. The sum of the interior angles is _____°. (Un triángulo tiene _____ vértices y _____ ángulos internos. La suma de la medida de los ángulos internos es _____°.)

Define polygon. (Define polígono.)

✂ cut on all dashed lines

▭ fold on all solid lines

Define cylinder. (Define cilindro.)

Define cone. (Define cono.)

cylinder

cone

✂ cut on all dashed lines   ⬓ fold on all solid lines

ilindro

O

Draw and label a net of the cylinder shown. (Dibuja el desarrollo del cilindro que se muestra. Señala sus partes.)

24 cm

14 cm

The formula for the volume of a cone is $V = \frac{1}{3}\pi r^2 h$. Find the volume of the cone shown. Round to the nearest tenth. (La fórmula para calcular el volumen de un cono es $V = \frac{1}{3}\pi r^2 h$. Calcula el volumen del cono que se muestra. Redondo a la décima más cercana.)

$V = $ _____

2 ft

7 ft

cut on all dashed lines

fold on all solid lines

Define sphere.
(Define esfera.)

To the nearest tenth find the volume of the hemisphere. (A la décima más cercana calcular el volumen de la semiesfera.)

8 mm

$V =$ _____

sphere

To the nearest tenth find the volume of the sphere. (A la décima más cercana calcular el volumen de la esfera.)

9 in.

$V =$ _____

hemisphere

a

ferio

List three examples of real-world objects that are spheres. (Menciona tres ejemplos de objetos reales que sean esferas.)

The formula for the volume of a sphere is $V = \frac{4}{3}\pi r^3$. What is the formula for the volume of a hemisphere? (La fórmula para calcular el volumen de una esfera es $V = \frac{4}{3}\pi r^3$. ¿Cuál es la fórmula para calcular el volumen de una semiesfera?)

$V = $ _____

esf

Define preimage. (Define preimagen.)

Define translation. (Define traslación.)

preimage

translation

Define image. (Define imagen.)

n

slación

pre

Triangle *ABC* is reflected over the x-axis. Label the image and the preimage. (El triángulo *ABC* se refleja sobre el eje x. Señala la imagen y la preimagen.)

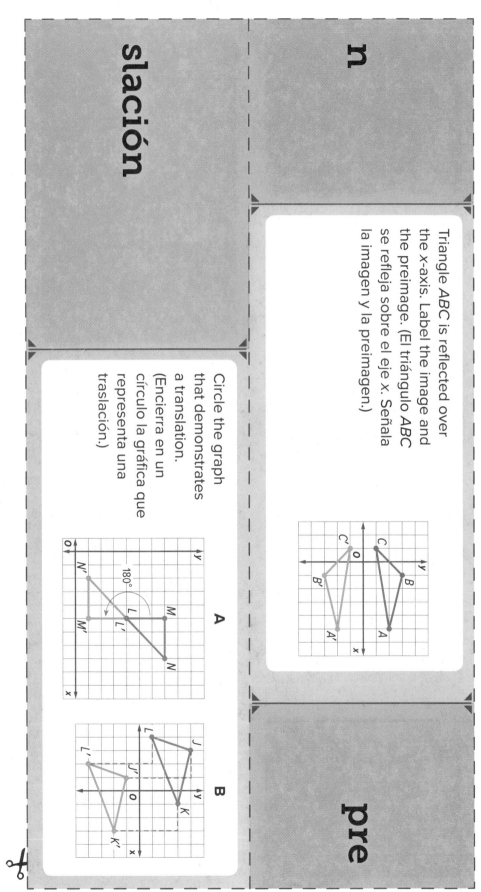

Circle the graph that demonstrates a translation. (Encierra en un círculo la gráfica que representa una traslación.)

A

B

Define transformation.
(Define transformación.)

transformation

Identify the line of reflection. (Identifica el línea de reflexión.)

line of reflection

ción

Describe the transformation shown in each figure.
(Describe la transformación que se muestra en cada figura.)

A

B

línea de reflexión

Circle the correct phrase to complete the sentence below.

In a reflection, the image is (congruent, not congruent) to the preimage.

(Encierra en un círculo la frase que completa correctamente la siguiente oración.

En un reflexión, la imagen (es congruente, no es congruente) con la preimagen.)

ángulo de

center of rotation

Circle the center of rotation. (Encierra en un círculo el centro de rotación.)

angle of

centro de rotación

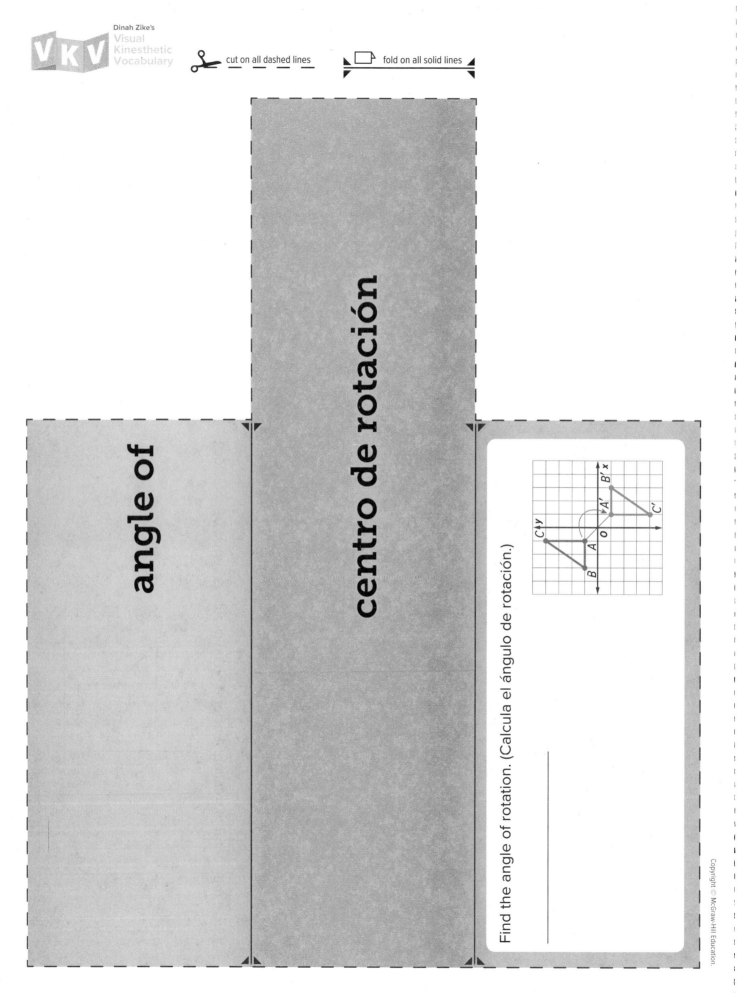

Find the angle of rotation. (Calcula el ángulo de rotación.)

_____

VKV Answer Appendix

VKV3

proportion: $x = 9.6$; two ratios or rates are equivalent
variación: yes; See students' work.

VKV4

nonproportional: A, C
variation: See students' graphs; yes; 70

VKV5

percent error: 25; $83\frac{1}{3}$; 1200; 90; See students' work.

VKV6

porcentaje de error: 13.9

VKV7

absolute value: See students' work for definition.
additive inverse: See students' work for definition; −13; 2; 25; −1

VKV8

valor absoluto: 23; 8; 17; 7
inverso aditivo: opposite

VKV9

rational number: See students' work for definition.

VKV10

número racional: Sample answer: fractional, repeating decimal, whole number.

VKV11

graph: Sample answer: draw a dot on the line at its location.
opposites: −12; 54; 16; −25

VKV12

graficar: See students' work for graphs.
opuestos: Sample answer: 6 and −6 are 6 are the same distance away from 0, but on opposite sides of 0 on the number line, therefore they are opposites.

VKV13

bar notation: Sample answers: It means that the 6 repeats forever; It would be impossible to continue writing a repeating decimal forever, so we have a symbol to show us that the number(s) repeat(s) forever.
common denominator: See students' work.

VKV14

notación de barra: $0.\overline{7}$; $9.3\overline{5}$; $-0.\overline{337}$
común denominador: $\frac{5}{40}$ and $\frac{8}{40}$

VKV15

exponente/base: See students' work for definitions.
irrational number: $\sqrt{8}$

VKV16

exponent/base: 6^5; 6; 5
rational: a fraction

VKV17

scientific notation: 2.75×10^5; 3×10^{-4}; See students' work.
perfect cube: −3; 6; 20; 27; 125
radical sign: 6; $\sqrt{}$

VKV18

cientifica notación: 2.63×10^5; 86,400
perfecto cubo: See students' work.
radical signo: indicate a positive square root

VKV19

coefficient: See students' work for definition.
factor: $3x$
factored form: The Distributive Property; See students' work.

VKV20

coeficiente: −5; 19; 9 and 17; 11
factorizar: $3(4x + 1)$; $3(9a + 4b)$; $2(8m - 9)$
forma factorizada: See students' work.

VKV21

linear expression: no; Sample answer: when a variable is squared, the graph of the expression does not form a straight line.
monomial: $3x$

VKV22

expresión lineal: Sample answer: $x + 3, 4y - 7$
monomio: See students' work for definition.

VKV23

equivalent equation: $x - 5 = 4$; $3 + x = 12$
solution: 5

VKV24

equación equivalente: Sample answer: yes; the equation $x + 11 = 14$ can be simplified to $x = 3$.
solución: 20; 8

VKV25

multiplicative inverse: $\frac{7}{2}$; $\frac{9}{5}$ or $\frac{18}{10}$

identity: $12p + 6 = 6 + 12p$

VKV26

inverso multiplicativo: 1
identidad: true for every value of the variable

VKV27

linear relationship: See students' work for both exercises.

VKV28

lineal relación: Sample answer: a straight line

VKV29

simulation: See students' work for definition.

VKV30

simulación: See students' work.

VKV31

theoretical probability: $\frac{1}{6}$

VKV32

probabilidad teórica: $\frac{4}{18}$ or $\frac{2}{9}$

VKV33

population: See students' work for definition.

VKV34

población: customers at a store; Sample answer: every third customer who walks through the front door
estadística: collecting; organizing; interpreting

VKV35

scale model: $\frac{1}{20}$

VKV36

modelo a escala: See students' work for examples.

VKV37

center: See students' work for definition.
circle: See students' work for definition.

VKV38

centro: See students' work.
circumference: about 47.1 m

VKV39

composite figure: See students' work for definition; See students' work.
diameter: twice
radius: diameter, circumference, area

VKV40

figura compuesto: See students' drawings.
diámetro: See students' work.
radio: See students' work.

VKV41

lateral surface area: See students' work for definition.
semicircle: $A = \frac{1}{2}\pi r^2$ or $\frac{\pi r^2}{2}$

VKV42

area de superficie lateral: 480 m^2
semicírculo: about 307.72 yd^2

VKV43

cone: Sample answer: cones and cylinders have faces that are circles and polyhedron must have only faces that are polygons.
congruent: See students' work for definition.
plane: 6

VKV44

congruente: 38°

plano: Sample answer: a plane extends in all directions forever, therefore it does not have edges to make a shape.

VKV45

regular pyramid: polygon

VKV46

pirámide regular: See students' work for definition.

VKV47

regular polygon: See students' work for drawing.

triangle: 1; 3

VKV48

polígono: See students' work.

triángulo: 3; 3; 180

VKV49

cone: See students' work.

cylinder: See students' work.

VKV50

cono: 29.3 ft³

cilindro: See students' work.

VKV51

hemisphere: 1,071.8 mm³

sphere: 3,053.6 in³; See students' work.

VKV52

hemisferio: $V = \frac{2}{3}\pi r^3$

esfera: Sample answer: basketball, globe, orange

VKV53

preimage: See students' work for both exercises.

translation: See students' work.

VKV54

preimagen: See students' work.

translación: B

VKV55

line of reflection: y-axis

transformation: See students' work.

VKV56

línea de reflexión: congruent

transformación: A: rotation; B: translation

VKV57

center of rotation: See students' work.

VKV58

angelo de rotación: 180°